D0688854

tea with Bea

tea with Bea

Bea's of Bloomsbury

photography by Kate Whitaker

RYLAND
PETERS
& SMALL

LONDON NEW YORK

Design, Photographic Art Direction
and Prop Stylist Steve Painter
Senior Editor Céline Hughes
Production Gordana Simakovic
Art Director Leslie Harrington
Publishing Director Alison Starling

Food Stylist Lucy Mckelvie
Indexer Hilary Bird

Company logo and wallpaper (on chapter openers)
designed by Colleen Jolly

First published in 2011 by
Ryland Peters & Small
20–21 Jockey's Fields
London WC1R 4BW
and
519 Broadway, 5th Floor
New York, NY 10012
www.rylandpeters.com

10 9 8 7 6 5 4 3 2 1

Text © Bea Vo 2011
Design and photographs
© Ryland Peters & Small 2011

Printed in China

The author's moral rights have been asserted.
All rights reserved. No part of this publication
may be reproduced, stored in a retrieval system,
or transmitted in any form or by any means, electronic,
mechanical, photocopying, or otherwise, without the
prior permission of the publisher.

ISBN: 978 1 84975 143 8

A CIP record for this book is available from
the British Library.

A CIP record for this book is available from
the Library of Congress.

Notes

• All spoon measurements are level, unless otherwise specified.

• All eggs are medium (for the UK) or large (for the US), unless otherwise specified. Uncooked or partially cooked eggs should not be served to the very young, the very old, those with compromised immune systems, or to pregnant women.

• When a recipe calls for the grated zest of citrus fruit, buy unwaxed fruit and wash well before using. If you can only find treated fruit, scrub well in warm soapy water and rinse before using.

• Baking sheets are frequently required to be lined with parchment paper throughout the book. It is recommended that silicone-based parchment paper be used.

• Ovens should be preheated to the specified temperature. Recipes in this book were tested using a fan-assisted oven. If using a regular oven, follow the manufacturer's instructions for adjusting temperatures. However, as a general rule, temperatures should be increased by about 15–20°C or about 35°F if using a regular oven.

contents

introduction

I should have known that I was meant to be a pastry chef when I looked back at my childhood and realized that the highlights had been baking for our academic club's bake sale, researching and baking special cheesecake muffins for my Jewish friend during Passover, and testing different colours of wet and dry caramel to see what works best with *crème caramel*. Also, I had an uncanny ability to get flour on the ceiling despite my diminutive size. At university, I spent more time in the kitchen than at the library and came to the conclusion that I needed to see if perhaps I should be on a different career track. I took a pastry course in the summer, loved every wonderful second of it, and decided that I needed to work in the real world of pastry to see if it was for me. I found an apprenticeship at Renee's Patisserie under Renee Senne, who took me under her wing. From there I moved into restaurants, learning at Nobu and Asia de Cuba in London.

Pastry is a craft which involves repetition and knowledge of techniques with your hands, and knowledge of how the ingredients will react in all sorts of environments. Eventually all that knowledge accumulates into the making of a pastry chef, who can not only create balanced desserts and is trained in the foundational techniques of the craft, but best of all, knows how to be a problem solver and fix things.

When I was first asked by the lovely Céline Hughes and Alison Starling at Ryland Peters & Small to write a cookbook, I was quite sceptical. After all, all of the greats have already covered almost every single possible recipe and technique there is to think of that we currently use in our own kitchens. But then it occurred to me that cookbooks aren't just textbooks – they are a reflection of a particular chef's point of view, much in the way that while we may have almost all types of stories told in novel form, we still look to seek new cadences and structure and ideas in an author's new work.

As a result, this book is meant to serve two purposes: one, to provide a more thorough understanding of basic pastry techniques, and two, to allow you to replicate our famous afternoon tea style for yourself. I hope the perspective of Bea's of Bloomsbury and the cadences in this book bring you success in your own kitchen.

Bea Vo

tips to a successful pastry run

The cookbook is extremely streamlined in its steps, which means you shouldn't miss one if you want a successful result.

1. Heat isn't the only thing to consider in the kitchen – cold plays an important role, too, particularly for a pastry chef. There is something in the belief that good pastry chefs must have cold hands to prevent things from melting when they shouldn't. And when a recipe asks you to chill something, there is a good reason for it and it's just as important as baking something in the oven!

2. Pastry requires patience. A lot of recipes need as little as 10 minutes to make, but you must also factor in prepping, chilling, baking and cooling times. One way to approach this book is to devote time to making lots of different things (which could take a whole day). Another approach is to fit the pastry making into your daily routine, so you're not tied to the cake pans. For example, while your pastry cream or your doughs are chilling, start making a quick pasta dinner or stir-fry. Pop things in the oven while you're clearing the table and you can have warm financiers or cookies ready for after dinner.

3. Baking is a craft: the more you do it, the better you get, so don't ever feel discouraged if your first try comes out funny. Cookbooks are like textbooks – they serve as guides but can't replace years of practice. You will learn techniques inherently and create your own tricks for success.

4. Electric stand mixers are a big investment but they're the best investments you'll make. I still have my home KitchenAid mixer and it's currently 13 years old and counting. Spread out over 13 years, that amounts to negligible sums. And the amount of time you'll save? Days and days...

5. Blowtorches are cool. That is all.

6. Many say it's really dangerous to alter recipes because they can come out badly, like a bad chemistry experiment. With regards to ratios of baking powder, sugar, salt, butter, eggs and liquid measures, they are on the ball. However, with things like adding spices and different chocolates, and playing with citrus zests, you can really be creative. The recipes in this book are foundational, so play around a bit until you find something that really works for you.

7. Don't overfill a piping bag – unless you like mixture all over your shirt in a nice straight line.

8. Having a proper oven thermometer is super-important. It's always best to make sure your oven isn't off by 25–30 degrees, which could drastically change the outcome of a recipe.

9. Best of all, remember that you are surrounded by sugar, butter and probably chocolate and fruit. Nibble some sugar when things look hairy.

making perfect tea

Tea is the essential part of afternoon tea and considering it's the most consumed beverage in the world (except for water), special attention must be paid to this wonderful brew. After all, imagine working hours and hours on special treats and desserts for a tea party only to serve it with dust found on a factory floor.

1. Always look for good, loose-leaf teas. Teas are made up of long leaves that are dried and processed. When whole, the essential oils are locked inside the tea and kept from oxidizing and tasting bitter.

2. Teas should be stored in an airtight, dark, cool container. Don't buy teas that come in boxes with open windows – the teas are already oxidized by the time you get them.

3. The trick with teas is to extract all of the lovely aromatics without extracting too many tannins, which cause bitterness. Match the temperatures and brewing times to your specific teas. Delicate teas like white or green teas require a lower temperature and longer brewing times; black teas will need a high temperature and slightly shorter brewing times.

4. Water quality is important – filtered water is always best.

5. Tea leaves need room to expand and move around. This makes most tea bags impractical because tea leaves don't have the space to expand and infuse the water properly. I recommend T-sacs, which are large, fillable bags because they're roomy and therefore suit teapots and mugs.

6. While loose-leaf teas can be expensive, the high quality of a tea means that the leaves can be infused over and over again. In fact, for many high-quality teas, the second, third and even later infusions are considered to be better than the first, which in some cultures is considered 'washing' the tea.

7. Teas will undergo many changes, even in the cup, over a period of time. While you're chatting with friends and eating yummy treats, take a moment to savour the tea you've so carefully made.

8. Recipe for tea: You will need 2–4 grams whole loose-leaf tea; 250 ml/1 cup filtered water; teapot; tea strainer for the cup; cup. Place tea inside the teapot. Boil the water and pour into the pot. For white tea, let the water sit for 1 minute before pouring into the pot, as you don't want it to be at boiling temperature. Let steep for 2 minutes (3 for white and herbal teas). At this point, you want to make sure the leaves have time to move freely in the water to fully expand and release the proper aromatics. Strain into cup. Add milk and sugar or honey and lemon as desired.

making perfect coffee

The perception of coffee we've grown up with is that it is a strong-smelling, deep, intense and bitter, dark brew and the perfect drink to get you through the morning. But coffee isn't just that – it can be just as varied as tea in its aromatics, colour, smell, and particularly in its bitterness or lack thereof.

1   Invest in freshly roasted beans from your local supplier. Beans shouldn't be any older than a few days old, and the expiration date on proper coffee beans is typically about a month (maximum).

2   Consider not just fairtrade: many artisanal roasters actually have better-than-fairtrade agreements with farmers, and by buying good-quality coffee, you are encouraging farmers to make better beans.

3   Always buy beans whole – coffee beans have wonderful aromatic oils that are released when crushed, but the oils are also very fragile. Crushed too soon, the oils will dissipate and even worse, can go rancid. Coffee beans should be ground only a few minutes before use.

4   Invest in a burr grinder; those same aromatic oils in coffee can be spoiled by high speed, uneven grinders. Invest in a good burr grinder, such as KitchenAid's Burr Grinder, or better yet, a Hario Skerton Coffee Mill that is just like a pepper mill, only for coffee!

5   Brewing times for coffee are just as important as baking times for cakes! Kitchen timers are good and useful.

6   My preferred method for brewing at home is the lovely French press. I was introduced to this device at the first French bistro I worked at and I continue to be in love with it.

7   Recipe for coffee: You will need 500 ml/1 cup filtered water; 30 g/1 oz. high-quality filter coffee beans; French press (500-ml/2-cup capacity); cup. Start to boil the water. Grind the coffee beans using either an electric burr grinder (e.g. KitchenAid) or a manual one (e.g. Hario Skerton Coffee Mill). You want a fairly coarse grind for filter coffee to allow for the extraction of the aromatics but not too much of the bitter oils. Pour into the French press. Add the boiling water. Stir with a spoon for a good 30 seconds to let the coffee grounds swell up and release their oils. Like tea, the grounds need to move for optimum infusion. Add the lid. Let sit for 3 minutes, before gently plunging. Pour into cup. Add milk and sugar as desired.

cookies & bars

ultimate chocolate chip cookies & double chocolate chip variation

The trick to the Ultimate Chocolate Chip Cookie is the obscene amount of butter and salt in the recipe – and of course, high-quality chocolate. The key to stuffing the cookie with lots of butter is chilling the dough until thoroughly chilled or frozen before baking to get the best spread and consistency. You can replace the vanilla extract with half a vanilla pod, but if doing so, add the vanilla pod seeds at the beginning with the butter and sugar to maximize the release of oils.

175 g/1¾ sticks unsalted butter, softened

½ teaspoon salt

40 g/2 tablespoons caster/superfine sugar

240 g/1 cup plus 2 tablespoons light brown soft sugar

1 egg

1 egg yolk

1½ teaspoons vanilla extract

240 g/1¾ cups plain/all-purpose flour

¼ teaspoon bicarbonate of/baking soda

25 ml/1 tablespoon milk

250 g/9 oz. high-quality dark/semi-sweet chocolate, chopped into pea-sized pieces

baking sheets, lined with parchment paper

makes about 20

Using an electric mixer with paddle or beater attachment (or an electric whisk), beat the butter, salt and both sugars until the mixture is lightened in colour, fluffy in texture and increases in volume.

Beat the egg and egg yolk together in a small bowl. Slowly mix into the butter mixture and beat until thoroughly combined. Add the vanilla extract and mix.

Sift together the flour and bicarbonate of/baking soda. Add half the flour mixture to the butter mixture and beat until just combined. Add the milk and beat until just combined. Add the remaining flour mixture and beat until just combined.

Add the chopped chocolate to the dough and mix until thoroughly combined.

Preheat the oven to 180°C (365°F) Gas 6.

Using 2 spoons or an easy-remove ice cream scoop, place large dollops of dough (about 40 g/1½ oz.) onto the prepared baking sheets, spaced well apart. (There's no need to flatten them and they will spread on baking.) Refrigerate for 20–25 minutes until thoroughly chilled. (At this point, you can also pop them in the freezer, freeze them for 2 hours, then place the dough balls in an airtight freezer bag and freeze for up to 2 weeks, for baking at a later date. Defrost for 15 minutes before baking.)

When the dough is thoroughly chilled, put the baking sheets in the preheated oven and bake for 9–13 minutes. The cookies are done when the tops don't look shiny or wet any more.

Remove from the oven and let cool on the baking sheets for 5 minutes. Please note: cookies keep baking on the sheets for about a minute after they're taken out of the oven and will be quite soft when hot but will harden when cool, so touching them to test their softness is not an accurate indication of doneness.

Transfer the cookies to a wire rack and let rest until ready to eat or eat them hot, straight out of the oven.

DOUBLE CHOCOLATE CHIP VARIATION: replace 2 tablespoons plain/all-purpose flour with 4 tablespoons natural cocoa powder and follow recipe as above.

snickerdoodles

Of all of the things that come from Amish country – whoopie pies, shoofly pie, funnel cakes and chow chow, to name a few – snickerdoodles hold the dearest place in my heart. Every year my family used to travel up to Lancaster County, Pennsylvania, to buy whole smoked hams, jars of chow chow and literally mountains of pretzels from the Tom Sturgis pretzel bakery. But my must-have item was always the buttery and cinnamony snickerdoodles.

225 g/2 sticks unsalted butter, softened
315 g/1½ cups plus 1 tablespoon caster/superfine sugar
2 eggs
1 teaspoon vanilla extract
350 g/2½ cups plain/all-purpose flour
2 teaspoons baking powder
½ teaspoon salt

for dipping
2 tablespoons ground cinnamon
300 g/1½ cups caster/superfine sugar

baking sheets, lined with parchment paper

makes about 24

Using an electric mixer with paddle or beater attachment (or an electric whisk), beat the butter and sugar until it turns almost white in colour and is light and fluffy.

Slowly incorporate the eggs, one at a time. Scrape down the batter from the side of the bowl and beat for another minute. Add the vanilla extract and mix.

Sift the flour, baking powder and salt together. With the mixer on slow speed, add the flour mixture to the butter mixture. Beat until just combined and a dough forms. Wrap the dough in clingfilm/plastic wrap and refrigerate for 15 minutes.

Meanwhile, mix the cinnamon and sugar, for dipping, in a shallow bowl.

Preheat the oven to 160°C (315°F) Gas 4.

Pull off pieces of dough the size of golf balls and roll into neat balls with your hands. Slightly flatten each ball into a disc with the palm of your hand and dip each thoroughly in the cinnamon sugar. Place on the prepared baking sheets, spaced apart.

Bake in the preheated oven for 13–16 minutes until the edges are slightly golden and the tops look dry and matt.

Remove from the oven and let cool on the baking sheets for 1 minute. Transfer the snickerdoodles to a wire rack and let rest until ready to eat or eat them hot, straight out of the oven.

lemon verbena semolina cookies

The dried lemon verbena provides a lovely, lemony earthiness to this recipe. If you use fresh, add a little extra to make sure you have enough essential oils. The rich olive oil is a perfect counterpoint to the zesty lemon. The cookies keep quite well in an airtight container for up to 1 week, so are perfect to keep on hand when friends come by for a spot of tea.

grated zest and freshly squeezed juice of 1 unwaxed lemon

½ teaspoon dried lemon verbena tea leaves

200 g/1 cup caster/superfine sugar, plus extra for dipping

¼ teaspoon salt

110 g/1 stick unsalted butter, softened

1½ tablespoons extra virgin olive oil

2 eggs

1 egg yolk

1 tablespoon vanilla extract or ½ vanilla pod, seeds only

280 g/2 cups plain/all-purpose flour, sifted

140 g/1 cup fine semolina (you can use coarse, but you will need to add 2 tablespoons plain/all-purpose flour to absorb more liquid)

1 teaspoon baking powder

¼ teaspoon bicarbonate of/baking soda

baking sheets, lined with parchment paper

makes about 20

Using an electric mixer with paddle or beater attachment (or an electric whisk), mix together the lemon zest, tea leaves, sugar and salt, and beat until the sugar smells very lemony – about 1 minute. The sugar will bruise the lemon zest and tea leaves, releasing the essential oils.

Add the butter, olive oil and lemon juice and beat until white and fluffy.

Beat the eggs and egg yolk together in a small bowl. Slowly mix into the butter mixture, beating continuously. Scrape down the batter from the side of the bowl and beat again until thoroughly combined. The mixture should look like a whipped, shiny mayonnaise. Add the vanilla extract and mix.

Mix the flour, semolina, baking powder and bicarbonate of/baking soda together. Tip straight into the butter mixture and stir until just combined.

The dough will be very soft. Still in the bowl, press it down with clingfilm/plastic wrap to remove any big air bubbles, cover well with the clingfilm/plastic wrap and refrigerate for 1 hour.

Preheat the oven to 170°C (340°F) Gas 5.

Pull off pieces of dough the size of golf balls and roll into neat balls with your hands. Dip them thoroughly in caster sugar and place on the prepared baking sheets, spacing them apart to allow for spreading during baking. Slightly flatten each ball into a disc with the palm of your hand.

Bake in the preheated oven for 12 minutes. The cookies should be a light golden colour and the tops should look dry and matt. Shininess is a sign of still-uncooked dough.

Remove from the oven and let cool on the baking sheets for 1 minute. Transfer the cookies to a wire rack and let rest for 20 minutes or until firm to the touch.

lavender shortbread

I always thought lavender was meant for soap, and only soap. And then I was introduced to the most marvellous lavender Earl Grey iced tea by chef Michael Katz at Le Cordon Bleu. While working in the savoury section during the hot summer months, on a second-floor kitchen with no air-conditioning and ridiculously hot stoves, the temperature easily reaching the high 30s (90s), he would run downstairs and concoct us this most refreshing drink. Lavender shortbread is so proper and perfect for afternoon tea with a pot of Earl Grey. Because there are so few ingredients, I use the best of everything, including fine sea salt.

70 g/⅓ cup caster/superfine sugar, plus extra for sprinkling

2 tablespoons icing/confectioners' sugar

½ teaspoon dried lavender

¼ teaspoon fine sea salt

350 g/3 sticks unsalted butter, slightly softened, cubed

350 g/2½ cups plain/all-purpose flour

brownie/baking pan, 30 x 20 x 5 cm/ 12 x 8 x 2 inches, e.g. Silverwood Eyecatcher, baselined with parchment paper

makes 24 squares

Preheat the oven to 145°C (290°F) Gas 3.

Whiz both the sugars, the lavender and salt in an electric mixer with paddle attachment (or rub with your bare hands) until the lavender buds are bruised and the sugars smell of lavender.

Beat the butter into the sugar mixture until well combined. Fold in the flour until just combined.

Transfer the mixture to the prepared brownie pan and pat the dough down until well combined and level. Sprinkle caster sugar over the top.

Bake in the preheated oven for 40–55 minutes until the top is golden brown and the edges shrink from the pan edges.

Remove from the oven and let cool in the pan for 10 minutes. Remove from the pan and cut into 24 squares.

oatmeal coconut raisin cookies

I was first introduced to these cookies by Mommy dearest – my beloved sister's mother-in-law, who always had some type of cake, cookie or baked treat in her home whenever I visited on the weekends. I have modified the recipe and replaced shortening with butter; the result is a crispier and more moreish cookie, but a good compromise is half shortening and butter if you would like to have the soft cake-like quality as well. We have incorporated brown sugar into the recipe to keep the cookies almost as soft as shortening would.

250 g/2 sticks unsalted butter, softened

1 teaspoon salt

250 g/1¼ cups dark brown soft sugar

100 g/½ cup caster/superfine sugar

2 eggs, lightly beaten

2 teaspoons vanilla extract

250 g/1¾ cups plain/all-purpose flour

1 teaspoon bicarbonate of/baking soda

2 tablespoons milk

250 g/2 cups jumbo oats (don't use quick-cook oats, as they will get mushy!)

150 g/¾ cup sultanas or raisins

125 g/1 cup soft shredded coconut e.g. Baker's Angel Flake (do not replace with desiccated coconut)

baking sheets, lined with parchment paper

makes about 40

Preheat the oven to 170°C (340°F) Gas 5.

Using an electric mixer with paddle or beater attachment (or an electric whisk), beat the butter, salt and both sugars until the mixture is lightened in colour, fluffy in texture and increases in volume.

Slowly mix the eggs into the butter mixture and beat until thoroughly combined. Add the vanilla extract and mix.

Sift together the flour and bicarbonate of/baking soda. Add half the flour mixture to the butter mixture and beat until just combined. Add the milk and beat until just combined. Add the remaining flour mixture and beat until just combined.

Add the oats, sultanas and flaked coconut and mix until just combined.

Using 2 spoons or an easy-remove ice cream scoop, place large dollops of dough (about 40 g/1½ oz.) onto the prepared baking sheets. Slightly flatten each ball into a disc with the palm of your hand. Refrigerate for 5 minutes until thoroughly chilled. (At this point, you can also pop them in the freezer, freeze them for 2 hours, then place the dough balls in an airtight freezer bag and freeze for up to 2 weeks, for baking at a later date. Defrost for 15 minutes before baking.)

When the dough is slightly chilled, put the baking sheets in the preheated oven and bake for 9–13 minutes. The cookies are done when the tops don't look shiny or wet any more.

Remove from the oven and let cool on the baking sheets for 5 minutes. Please note: cookies keep baking on the sheets for about a minute after they're taken out of the oven and will be quite soft when hot but will harden when cool, so touching them to test their softness is not an accurate indication of doneness.

Transfer the cookies to a wire rack and let rest until ready to eat or eat them hot, straight out of the oven.

chocolate peanut butter biscotti

During the plans for opening the shop, I had to find a coffee supplier. I was spoiled with the joys of Gimme! Coffee during my university days, so finding an artisan coffee roaster for the shop was a priority. I was blessed to meet Anette Moldvaer and James Hoffmann of Square Mile Coffee and we became their first café clients. Anette's palate is so amazing. Their espresso blends have won 3 consecutive World Barista Championships and continue to be among the most desired beans in the world. So, what to have with a world-class coffee? Chocolate Peanut Butter Biscotti, of course. So says the American.

300 g/2 cups plain/all-purpose flour

1½ teaspoons baking powder

1½ teaspoons salt

100 g/½ cup light brown soft sugar

40 g/2 tablespoons natural cocoa powder (not Dutch-process)

40 g/2 tablespoons golden syrup

3 tablespoons sunflower oil

2 eggs

2 teaspoons water

1 teaspoon vanilla extract

80 g/⅔ cup shelled whole peanuts (unsalted or honey roasted)

80 g/3 oz. high-quality dark/semi-sweet chocolate, chopped into pea-sized pieces

caster/superfine sugar, for sprinkling

70 g/⅓ cup peanut butter (crunchy or smooth)

baking sheet, lined with parchment paper

makes about 30

Put the flour, baking powder, salt, sugar and cocoa powder in a large mixing bowl and mix until well combined.

Put the golden syrup, oil, eggs, water and vanilla extract in a separate bowl and whisk until well combined. Add to the dry mixture and mix until just combined and no trace of dry flour remains.

Add the peanuts and chocolate and incorporate until just combined.

Bring the dough together into a ball, wrap in clingfilm/plastic wrap and refrigerate for 1 hour.

Preheat the oven to 145°C (290°F) Gas 3.

Sprinkle the work surface liberally with caster sugar. Transfer the dough to the work surface and flatten roughly with your hands. Dot spoonfuls of peanut butter all over the dough. Lightly roll the dough into a log about 6 cm/2½ inches wide and 2 cm/1 inch high (it will spread when baking). Try to encase the peanut butter inside the log, as it can burn if exposed directly to the heat of the oven.

Place the log on the prepared baking sheet and bake in the preheated oven for 25–40 minutes until the top is completely hardened, and when tapped, feels sturdy and not squishy inside. Remove from the oven and let cool for 30 minutes. Turn the oven temperature down to 135°C (265°F) Gas 2.

Slice the cooled log, diagonally, into 1-cm/½-inch wide batons.

Lay all the batons flat on the same baking sheet and bake for 10–15 minutes until nice and dry, then flip all the biscotti over and bake again for 10–15 minutes. Remove from the oven and let cool on the baking sheet for 1 minute.

Transfer the biscotti to a wire rack and let cool completely. Store in airtight container for up to 1 month.

nutty lemon biscotti

These biscotti are great, as they contain no butter or milk, so they suit those with certain types of dairy allergies. They're also a one-bowl wonder, which makes things easy and they last for quite a long time! The olive oil also allows the biscotti to have a wonderful airy crumb and provides an unctuous mouthfeel. You can also play with the basic dough and add different combinations, such as lemon with dried sour cherries, dried apricots and white chocolate.

100 g/½ cup caster/superfine sugar, plus extra for sprinkling

grated zest and freshly squeezed juice of 1 large unwaxed lemon

350 g/2½ cups plain/all-purpose flour

1½ teaspoons baking powder

1½ teaspoons salt

a pinch of ground cardamom

40 g/2 tablespoons honey

2 eggs

3 tablespoons extra virgin olive oil

1 teaspoon vanilla extract

50 g/¼ cup shelled, unsalted whole pistachios

50 g/⅓ cup shelled, blanched whole hazelnuts

50 g/¼ cup shelled whole almonds

baking sheet, lined with parchment paper

makes about 30

Whiz the sugar and lemon zest in an electric mixer with paddle attachment (or rub with your bare hands) until the sugar smells tart and lemony.

Add the flour, baking powder and salt, and stir until well combined.

Put the lemon juice, ground cardamom, honey, eggs, olive oil and vanilla extract in a separate bowl and whisk until well combined. Add to the dry mixture and mix until just combined and no trace of dry flour remains.

Add the pistachios, hazelnuts and almonds, and incorporate until just combined. The dough will be sticky!

Bring the dough together into a ball, wrap in clingfilm/plastic wrap and refrigerate for 1 hour.

Preheat the oven to 145°C (290°F) Gas 3.

Sprinkle the work surface liberally with caster sugar. Transfer the dough to the work surface and lightly roll or shape it into a log about 6 cm/2½ inches wide and 2 cm/1 inch high (it will spread when baking).

Place the log on the prepared baking sheet and bake in the preheated oven for 25–40 minutes until the top is completely hardened and, when tapped, feels sturdy and not squishy inside. Remove from the oven and let cool for 30 minutes. Turn the oven temperature down to 135°C (265°F) Gas 2.

Slice the cooled log, diagonally, into 1-cm/½-inch wide batons.

Lay all the batons flat on the same baking sheet and bake for 10–15 minutes until nice and dry, then flip all the biscotti over and bake again for 10–15 minutes. Remove from the oven and let cool on the baking sheet for 1 minute.

Transfer the biscotti to a wire rack and let cool completely. Store in airtight container for up to 1 month.

rocky road fudge bars

I was asked to create a bar cookie that is ultimate Americana. We had some leftover off-cuts of our Vanilla Marshmallows (see page 59) and I instantly thought: rocky road. By incorporating a shortbread base, it has that British touch as well. My preferred beverage to accompany a Rocky Road Fudge Bar? Hot chocolate with whipped cream. If you're going to indulge, go all the way.

80 g/⅔ cup roasted blanched almonds

12 large vanilla marshmallows, chopped into 1.5-cm/½-inch cubes

shortbread base

120 g/⅔ cup caster/superfine sugar

500 g/4¼ sticks unsalted butter, slightly softened

500 g/3½ cups plain/all-purpose flour

a pinch of salt

fudge filling

150 g/1¼ sticks unsalted butter

100 g/⅛ cup golden syrup

150 ml/⅔ cup whipping cream

150 g/5½ oz. high-quality dark/semi-sweet chocolate, chopped into chunks

500 g/2½ cups caster/superfine sugar

1 teaspoon vanilla extract

brownie/baking pan, 30 x 20 x 5 cm/ 12 x 8 x 2 inches, e.g. Silverwood Eyecatcher, greased and lined with parchment paper

sugar thermometer

makes about 24 small or 12 large

Preheat the oven to 170°C (340°F) Gas 5.

To make the shortbread base, beat the sugar and butter until well combined. Fold in the flour and salt until just combined.

Transfer the mixture to the prepared brownie pan and pat the dough down until well combined and level. Refrigerate for 5 minutes.

Bake in the preheated oven for 18–25 minutes until the top is golden brown and the edges shrink from the pan edges.

Remove from oven and let cool.

While the shortbread base is cooling, make the fudge filling. Put the butter, golden syrup, cream, chocolate and sugar into a large saucepan. Add the sugar thermometer and cook over medium heat until the temperature on the thermometer reaches 100°C/212°F. Stir occasionally.

When the mixture looks homogeneous, brush the inside of the saucepan with clean water to dislodge any stray grains of sugar. Keep cooking over medium heat to bring to soft ball stage, 120°C/248°F.

When the fudge reaches 120°C/248°F, remove from the heat and pour into a large, metal mixing bowl. Stir in the vanilla extract and continue stirring until the fudge cools down and loses its glossiness. This can take a few minutes.

While still warm and pourable, pour the fudge on top of the shortbread base and let sit for 4 minutes. Before it completely sets, sprinkle the almonds and marshmallows on top and press in slightly. Let cool completely.

When cool, remove from the pan and cut into 24 small or 12 large squares.

TIP: to help you line the brownie pan, cut 2–4-cm/1–2-inch diagonal incisions, pointing towards the middle, at each corner of the parchment paper and the paper will fit more snugly in the pan.

granola bars

Granola bars are the type of treat that have an aura of being healthy, but that are ultimately a wonderful vehicle for sugar. This bar embraces that by having three types of sugar – honey, golden syrup and demerara sugar – to provide the sweetening and binding. The orange and dried cherries add a refreshing counterpoint to the sweetness, while the coconut and nuts just give the perfect crunch. The oats are the ideal excuse to enjoy this sweet treat for brekkie.

125 g/1 stick unsalted butter

150 g/½ cup honey

100 g/⅓ cup golden syrup

250 g/1 cup plus 1 tablespoon demerara sugar

freshly squeezed juice and grated zest of 1 orange

1 teaspoon vanilla extract

300 g/2½ cups jumbo oats (not quick-cook oats)

200 g/1½ cups desiccated coconut

125 g/1½ cups flaked/slivered almonds

200 g/1¾ cups shelled whole pecans

100 g/¾ cup shelled peanuts (unsalted)

100 g/¾ cup dried sour cherries

2 brownie/baking pans, 30 x 20 x 5 cm/12 x 8 x 2 inches, e.g. Silverwood Eyecatcher, lined with parchment paper

makes 48 squares

Preheat the oven to 135°C (265°F) Gas 2.

Put the butter, honey, golden syrup, sugar and orange juice in a saucepan and bring to a boil. Remove from the heat.

Combine the remaining ingredients in a large mixing bowl.

Slowly pour the molten sugar syrup into the dry ingredients in the mixing bowl and stir to combine. Be very careful, as it is very, very hot!

Divide the mixture between the brownie pans and, using a greased palette knife, gently press down the granola mixture.

Bake in the preheated oven for 30–45 minutes until golden brown.

Remove from the oven and let rest in the pans for 10–15 minutes, or until slightly warm to the touch.

While still warm, gently tip the mixture out of the pans and cut each into 24 squares. Store in an airtight container for up to 2 weeks.

TIP: to change this recipe from bars to granola for eating with yogurt, reduce the demerara sugar down to 200 g/1 scant cup, and loosely bake in the brownie pans. Stir every 15 minutes in the oven with a wooden spoon to keep the oats loose and to evenly bake the granola. After the pans are out of the oven, stir again every 10 minutes until cool to separate the granola pieces. If you miss this step you will end up with a hard rock of granola.

killer Valrhona brownies

These brownies are ridiculously fudgy due to the high chocolate and sugar content. The extra sugar also creates that lovely crust on top. They must undergo a freezing process to preserve their gooeyness, yet still be easy to cut.

250 g/9 oz. high-quality dark/semi-sweet chocolate couverture (we recommend Valrhona Caraïbe 66%, Scharffen Berger 62% or Green & Blacks Organic 70%), chopped into pea-sized pieces

250 g/2 sticks plus 2 tablespoons unsalted butter

4 eggs

½ teaspoon salt

250 g/1¼ cups dark brown soft sugar

250 g/1¼ cups caster/superfine sugar

250 g/1¼ cups plain/all-purpose flour, sifted

30 g/⅓ cup soft shredded coconut e.g. Baker's Angel Flake (do not replace with desiccated coconut)

30 g/⅓ cup pecan halves or pieces

30 g/⅓ cup shelled, blanched whole hazelnuts

100 g/¾ cup peanut butter (crunchy or smooth)

50 g/⅓ cup storebought dulce de leche (or to make your own, see page 136)

square 23-cm/9-inch baking pan, 7 cm/ 3 inches deep, greased and lined with parchment paper

makes about 16 small or 9 large squares

Preheat the oven to 180°C (365°F) Gas 6.

Put the chocolate in a medium bowl. Put the butter in a saucepan and bring to a strong boil. Pour the butter immediately over the chocolate and stir with a wooden spoon until well combined and glossy.

Put the eggs, salt and both sugars in a large mixing bowl and immediately stir with a wooden spoon until combined. Don't let the eggs and sugar sit in the same bowl by themselves for long, otherwise the sugar will cook the egg into tiny bits of scrambled egg. (This is because sugar is hydroscopic, meaning that it loves to absorb water, thereby drying out the eggs and effectively cooking them if left alone with them.)

Pour the warm chocolate mixture into the egg mixture. Stir until well mixed.

Fold the flour into the chocolate mixture until just combined. Do not overmix, otherwise the brownies will be less fudgy and more bread-like.

Transfer the mixture to the prepared brownie pan and immediately scatter the coconut, pecans and hazelnuts over the top. Spread them out and push them down with a spatula until level, and make sure the nuts are covered in brownie mixture so that they don't burn in the oven.

Add dollops of the peanut butter and dulce de leche all over the brownie. Using a table knife, lightly swirl the peanut butter and dulce de leche into the brownie mixture so that it's evenly distributed. Do not overmix, as streaks of peanut butter and dulce de leche are desirable.

Bake in the preheated oven for 10 minutes, then quickly reduce the oven temperature to 160°C (340°F) Gas 4 and leave the oven door open for 30 seconds to cool down. Bake for an additional 15 minutes or until the top of the brownie shows no trace of shiny spots.

Remove from the oven and let cool in the pan, on a wire rack, for 10 minutes. Immediately place in the freezer for 1 hour. (You can also keep them in the freezer for up to 2 weeks.)

Remove the brownie from the pan and cut into 16 small or 9 large squares. Store in an airtight container for 3 days.

Belgian blondies

If you are not a fan of white chocolate, you will still like these. If you are a fan of white chocolate, you will love these. The unique structure of white chocolate allows the batter to stay quite gooey even when cooked. It is essential to have real white chocolate as opposed to 'white chocolate product', which will clump up and separate in an oily mess when melted with butter.

480 g/1 lb. good-quality white chocolate, chopped into pea-sized pieces

320 g/2¾ sticks unsalted butter

2 eggs

250 g/1¼ cups caster/superfine sugar

1 teaspoon vanilla extract

250 g/1¾ cups plain/all-purpose flour

a pinch of salt

brownie/baking pan, 30 x 20 x 5 cm/ 12 x 8 x 2 inches, e.g. Silverwood Eyecatcher, greased and lined with parchment paper

makes 12

Preheat the oven to 170°C (340°F) Gas 5.

Put the chocolate in a medium bowl. Put the butter in a saucepan and bring to a boil. Pour the butter immediately over the chocolate and stir with a wooden spoon until well combined.

Put the eggs, sugar and vanilla extract in a large mixing bowl and whisk together. Pour the warm chocolate mixture into the egg mixture and stir. Add the flour and salt and mix until just combined.

Transfer the mixture to the prepared brownie pan and bake in the preheated oven for 28–33 minutes. It should be golden brown on top and still gooey in the centre, so a wooden skewer test will not work.

Remove from the oven and let cool in the pan for 1 hour. Refrigerate for 2 hours. Remove the blondie from the pan and cut into 12 squares.

TIP: make sure you use real, high-quality white chocolate and not white chocolate baking drops. White chocolate consists of milk, sugar and cocoa butter, while white baking drops are made of vegetable oil, weird flavouring, sugar and some type of milk product: a no-no in baking.

scones & small treats

the ultimate afternoon tea scone

The most important thing in a scone recipe is not the quantity of ingredients or even what's in it – it's the method. Follow this method for any scone recipe, and it will be gold. The most crucial part of the scone is the interplay between the butter, flour and temperature. Butter is made primarily of fat and water. What you want is for butter to stay in a nice cold form so that the fat won't melt and release water prematurely before it hits the oven. If the butter does melt, water will interact with the flour molecules and make gluten, toughening the scone. In addition, you want the butter to be as cold as possible before it goes into a hot preheated oven – this way, instead of the butter melting into the flour, it instantly makes steam, which results in a light, puffy, flaky scone.

600 g/4¼ cups plain/all-purpose flour

75 g/⅓ cup caster/superfine sugar

¼ teaspoon salt

5 teaspoons baking powder

240 g/2 sticks unsalted butter, cut into 1-cm/½-inch cubes and chilled for at least 10 minutes

2 eggs

120 ml/½ cup milk

150 ml/⅔ cup whipping cream

round cookie cutter in the size of your choice

baking sheets, lined with parchment paper

makes about 24

Put the flour, sugar, salt and baking powder in a large mixing bowl (or in an electric mixer with paddle attachment) and stir with a wooden spoon until well combined. Add the cold butter and rub between your fingertips (or in the mixer with the paddle attachment) until you reach a sand-like consistency. Refrigerate for 10 minutes.

Put the eggs, milk and cream in a separate bowl and beat lightly. Refrigerate for 10 minutes.

Preheat the oven to 180°C (365°F) Gas 6. Preheating is crucial!

Fold the egg mixture into the sandy flour mixture until just combined and no bits of dryness remain. (As soon as you add any form of liquid to any dough, keep in mind that the flour will automatically want to make gluten with liquids, and the best way to prevent that is to keep the dough from being overworked or warming up.) The dough should be quite wet and, when pulled apart, break off in clumps and not stretch. Refrigerate for 10 minutes.

Flour your work surface and rolling pin liberally. Flip your cold dough on the surface. Don't knead! Liberally flour the top of the dough. Roll the dough to about the height of the cookie cutter you're using. Dip the cutter in flour and use to cut a round from the dough. Transfer to the prepared baking sheet. Continue cutting out rounds, then gather up the off-cuts and gently re-ball and re-roll to cut out more.

Put the scones immediately into the preheated oven for 8 minutes if you have small, skinny scones, and 10 minutes if you have big, fat ones.

After the time has elapsed, turn the oven down to 170°C (340°F) Gas 5 and let the scones bake for another 8–14 minutes. How do you know a scone is done? It has a lovely golden colour, will have risen quite a bit and will spring back when pressed lightly. Serve warm with clotted cream and strawberry jam on the day of baking.

orange cranberry scones

These American-style scones have so much butter and cream and fruit – and flavour – that it's almost impossible to cut them into perfect little shapes. The recommended way to deal with this super-rich and sticky dough is to cut it into triangular pie-slice shapes with a bench scraper, refrigerate and then move the pieces gently around the baking sheet and bake. The best accompaniment to these scones is butter and a bit of Seville orange marmalade – a perfect complement to the dried cranberries.

60 g/5 tablespoons caster/superfine sugar, plus extra for sprinkling

grated zest of 1 orange

530 g/3¾ cups plain/all-purpose flour

1½ teaspoons baking powder

½ teaspoon salt

350 g/3 sticks unsalted butter, cut into pea-sized cubes and chilled

3 eggs

1 egg yolk

185 ml/¾ cup whipping cream

100 g/¾ cup dried cranberries

baking sheet, lined with parchment paper

makes about 12

Whiz the sugar and orange zest in an electric mixer with paddle attachment (or rub with your bare hands) until the sugar smells citrussy.

Add the flour, baking powder and salt and stir.

Add the cold butter to the flour mixture and rub between your fingertips (or in the mixer with paddle attachment) until you reach a sand-like consistency. Refrigerate for 20 minutes.

Preheat the oven to 170°C (340°F) Gas 5.

Put the whole eggs, egg yolk and cream in a separate bowl and beat lightly. Pour into the sandy flour mixture and add the cranberries. Fold until just combined. Be careful not to overmix at this stage, to ensure the scones stay nice and soft. Keep in mind that the dough will be quite soft and sticky.

Sprinkle the baking sheet liberally with caster sugar.

Flip the dough out onto the baking sheet and sprinkle caster sugar on top. Pat down into a disc about 3 cm/1¼ inches high.

Using a sharp, serrated knife, cut the dough disc into fat wedges like a pie, and space them apart on the baking sheet. Bake in the preheated oven for 25–30 minutes until golden brown and solid when pressed.

Serve warm. Scones are best eaten on the day of baking.

gingerbread Guinness cupcakes

Having an Austrian chef for a husband means two things: you must love Lebkuchen and you must love beer. These cupcakes fulfil both desires. If you like ginger, you will love this cake. The Guinness stout adds earthiness to the cake and also reacts with the baking soda to make a beautiful soft and moist crumb. It works well as both a cake and cupcake, and if you're feeling particularly playful, the best decorations are mini gingerbread men sprinkles.

250 ml/1 cup Guinness stout

250 g/¾ cup black treacle/molasses

1½ teaspoons bicarbonate of/baking soda

280 g/2 cups plain/all-purpose flour

1½ teaspoons baking powder

1 tablespoon ground ginger

1 teaspoon ground cinnamon

¼ teaspoon ground allspice

¼ teaspoon freshly grated nutmeg

¼ teaspoon ground cardamom

¼ teaspoon ground cloves

3 eggs

100 g/½ cup caster/superfine sugar

100 g/½ cup dark brown soft sugar

1 tablespoon finely grated peeled fresh ginger

200 ml/¾ cup sunflower oil

chopped crystallized ginger, to decorate

golden cream cheese icing

225 g/1 cup cream cheese

60 g/3 tablespoons unsalted butter, softened

175 g/1½ cups icing/confectioners' sugar, sifted

1 teaspoon vanilla extract

2 tablespoons golden syrup

muffin trays, lined with about 24 large cupcake cases

piping bag fitted with a star-shaped nozzle/tip

makes 24

Preheat the oven to 170°C (340°F) Gas 5.

Put the Guinness and treacle in a tall saucepan (the next step will cause the mixture to bubble up violently and potentially overflow, so choose a very tall pan) and bring to a boil over high heat. Remove from the heat and stir in the bicarbonate of/baking soda. Let stand until completely cool.

Put the flour, baking powder, ground ginger, cinnamon, allspice, nutmeg, cardamom and cloves in a bowl and stir until well blended.

In a separate bowl, combine the eggs, both sugars and the grated fresh ginger. Gradually add the oil. Add the stout syrup and stir thoroughly.

Add the egg mixture to the dry ingredients and mix until just combined.

Spoon the mixture into the prepared cupcake cases, filling them four-fifths of the way up (the mixture will not rise that much).

Bake in the preheated oven for 25–35 minutes until they feel springy to the touch. Remove the cupcakes from the muffin tray and let cool on a wire rack.

To make the golden cream cheese icing, put the cream cheese and butter in a bowl and beat until combined and glossy. Add the icing/confectioners' sugar and beat until fluffy. Fold in the vanilla extract and golden syrup.

Fill the prepared piping bag with the icing and pipe onto the cupcakes. Top with a couple of pieces of crystallized ginger, to decorate.

VARIATION: to make into a layer cake instead of cupcakes, spoon the mixture into 2 x 20-cm/8-inch pans or 1 x 25-cm/10-inch pan and bake at 160°C (315°F) Gas 4 for 45–55 minutes (for the small pans) or 1 hour 15 minutes (for the large pan).

blueberry streusel muffins

Muffins are great because they're an own-bowl wonder. I consider them to also be a 'vehicle of fruit.' A high fruit-to-cake ratio is a must. Moreover, muffins should be eaten the moment baked – the difference between a freshly baked muffin and one that's eight hours old is astounding. If you want the oversized muffin tops you see in the cafés, just grease your muffin tray beforehand to prevent sticking, then add more batter to each muffin case.

225 g/1½ cups plain/all-purpose flour, plus 1 tablespoon for coating the blueberries

200 g/1 cup caster/superfine sugar

1½ teaspoons baking powder

¼ teaspoon salt

50 ml/3 tablespoons milk

40 ml/2 tablespoons double/heavy cream

2 eggs

65 g/4 tablespoons unsalted butter, melted

250 g/2½ cups blueberries, fresh or frozen

streusel topping

200 g/1½ cups plain/all-purpose flour

70 g/⅓ cup dark brown soft sugar

70 g/⅓ cup caster/superfine sugar

125 g/1 stick chilled butter, cut into 1-cm/½-inch cubes and chilled

2 teaspoons ground cinnamon

1 teaspoon vanilla extract

12-hole muffin tray, lined with muffin cases

makes 12

Preheat the oven to 180°C (365°F) Gas 6.

Put the flour, sugar, baking powder and salt in a large mixing bowl and stir until well blended.

In a separate bowl, combine the milk, cream and eggs. Pour into the flour mixture and stir until just combined. Fold in the melted butter.

In another bowl, toss the blueberries in the extra flour until thoroughly coated, then fold into the muffin batter.

Spoon the mixture into the prepared muffin cases, filling them four-fifths of the way up.

To make the streusel topping, combine all ingredients and rub with your fingers until nice crumbly, pea-sized balls form. Refrigerate for 10 minutes.

Scatter the streusel topping over the muffins.

Bake in the preheated oven for 25–35 minutes. A wooden skewer inserted in the middle should come out dry and crumbly, and the tops of the muffins should feel springy to the touch. Remove the muffins from the muffin tray and eat immediately.

almond cherry muffins

These muffins are kind of a play on the friand, the popular French/Australian treat, and the wonderful muffin. The yogurt and ground almonds add a bit of lightness to the crumb and the tart cherries will wake you up in the morning.

240 g/1¼ cups caster/superfine sugar

grated zest of 1 unwaxed lemon

150 g/1 cup plain/all-purpose flour, plus 1 tablespoon for coating the cherries

70 g/½ cup ground almonds

2 teaspoons baking powder

a pinch of salt

3 eggs

130 g/½ cup Greek yogurt

½ teaspoon vanilla extract

¼ teaspoon almond extract

80 ml/⅓ cup sunflower oil

50 g/3½ tablespoons unsalted butter, melted

120 g/1¼ cups pitted sour cherries

about 50 g/⅔ cup flaked/slivered almonds, for sprinkling

12-hole muffin tray, lined with muffin cases

makes 16

Preheat the oven to 170°C (340°F) Gas 5.

Whiz the sugar and lemon zest in an electric mixer with paddle attachment (or rub with your bare hands) until the sugar smells super lemony.

Add the flour, ground almonds, baking powder and salt and mix well.

In a separate bowl, combine the eggs, yogurt and vanilla and almond extracts. Pour into the flour mixture and stir until just combined and no traces of flour remain. Fold in the oil and melted butter.

In another bowl, toss the cherries in the extra flour until thoroughly coated, then fold into the muffin batter.

Spoon the mixture into the prepared muffin cases and scatter the almonds over the tops. Bake in the preheated oven for 20–28 minutes. A wooden skewer inserted in the middle should come out dry and crumbly, and the tops of the muffins should feel springy to the touch. Remove the muffins from the muffin tray and eat immediately.

doughnut muffins

I love doughnuts. I remember them from when I was four years old, and my sister would stick me in the back seat of the car in the middle of the night and head on an hour-long journey to the regional Krispy Kreme bakery. You see, back when Krispy Kreme Doughnuts was a small regional company, Krispy Kreme Doughnuts were only available hot from the hours of 1 a.m. to 4 a.m., before they went to the local supermarkets and before they had those posh stores you now see everywhere. So doughnuts are in my blood. But I also fell in love with cake doughnuts when we visited Amish country in Lancaster, Pennsylvania, with a soft crumb and touches of nutmeg. Owning a deep fat fryer at home is out of the question for us, so what to do? These doughnut muffins are the answer, and a popular blog idea that should stand the test of time.

420 g/3 cups plain/all-purpose flour

4 teaspoons baking powder

½ teaspoon salt

½ teaspoon freshly grated nutmeg

330 g/1⅔ cups caster/superfine sugar

2 eggs, lightly beaten

375 ml/1½ cups buttermilk

2 teaspoons vanilla extract

130 ml/⅗ cup sunflower oil

coating & dipping

250 g/2 sticks unsalted butter, melted

300 g/1½ cups caster/superfine sugar

about ½ jar of raspberry jam

2 x 12-hole muffin trays, well greased

piping bag fitted with a plain nozzle/tip

makes about 22

Preheat the oven to 180°C (365°F) Gas 6.

Put all the dry ingredients in a bowl. Add all the wet ingredients and stir until just combined. Don't overmix.

Spoon the mixture into the muffin tray holes, filling them three quarters of the way up.

Bake in the preheated oven for 22–30 minutes. A wooden skewer inserted in the middle should come out dry and crumbly.

While the muffins are baking, put the melted butter and sugar in their own shallow bowls and set aside.

Remove the muffin trays from the oven and tip the muffins out. Immediately dip the muffins in the melted butter, then roll in the sugar to liberally and evenly coat.

Fill the prepared piping bag with jam. Push the nozzle/tip through the top (or bottom if you want it to look neater) of the doughnut, up to midway. Pipe about 1 tablespoon of jam inside each doughnut and serve immediately.

VARIATIONS

APPLE CINNAMON: add ½ teaspoon ground cardamom to the batter, and 2 teaspoons ground cinnamon to the caster sugar for coating. Fill with apple jam or compote.

COCONUT: replace the nutmeg with vanilla extract and fill with Coconut Pastry Cream (see page 83).

almond financiers & mocha variation

Everyone always talks of Proustian madeleines but I've always been a bigger fan of financiers. Done right, the *beurre noisette* or 'hazelnut butter' essentially fries the little biscuits until you have a nice crispy exterior and a soft cake-like middle. And they last for a couple of days if you keep them in an airtight container. The best thing is that they are also gluten-free, so they're suitable for those who can't have gluten. The mixture also freezes well, so pop the unused half (see recipe) in the oven whenever unexpected guests arrive (or a midnight snack is needed!)

250 g/2 sticks unsalted butter, plus extra for greasing

375 g/1¼ cups caster/superfine sugar

50 g/½ cup cornflour/cornstarch, plus extra for dusting

375 g/3 cups ground almonds

10 egg whites, lightly beaten

icing/confectioners' sugar, for dusting

mini-muffin trays, or special financier moulds

2 large piping bags and 1 plain nozzle/tip

makes about 48

To make the *beurre noisette*, put the butter in a large saucepan and cook over high heat until it reaches a boil. Lower the heat to medium–low and cook until most of the water has evaporated. Instead of smelling like cheese, it should start to smell like hazelnuts, and there should be small, brown crispy bits at the bottom of the pan. It can take anywhere from 10 minutes to 30 minutes.

Pour the liquid into a metal mixing bowl, being careful to leave the brown solids behind. Let cool for 20 minutes.

Put the sugar, cornflour/cornstarch and almonds in a large bowl and stir well. Fold in the egg whites until combined. Fold in the *beurre noisette*. Refrigerate for 2 hours.

In the meantime, grease the muffin trays or financier moulds and dust with cornflour/cornstarch. Grease again.

Preheat the oven to 180°C (365°F) Gas 6.

Fill one prepared piping bag with half the mixture and secure the ends with elastic bands to seal. Pop in the freezer and use in the future (defrost for 30 minutes before baking).

Fill the other prepared piping bag, fitted with a plain nozzle/tip, with the remaining mixture, and pipe each mini-muffin dimple almost to the top.

Bake in the preheated oven for 10 minutes, then lower the oven temperature to 170°C (340°F) Gas 5. Bake for another 7–15 minutes until the tops are golden brown and feel springy to the touch.

Remove from the oven and let rest for 1 minute before popping out of the trays. Dust with icing/confectioners' sugar before serving.

MOCHA VARIATION: start the recipe as above, adding 1 tablespoon freshly ground coffee to the *beurre noisette* when you take it off the heat. After letting cool for about 20 minutes, strain it. Continue with the recipe, replacing the cornflour/cornstarch with cocoa powder. Dust cocoa powder over the baked financiers before serving.

raspberry meringues

Raspberry meringues always seem to have the wow factor – little puffy clouds of sugar coloured brightly in red. Here's how you make them – crispy outside and gooey inside. Absolutely irresistible, they are the perfect confection for afternoon tea. If you like purple, blackcurrant purée will do the trick as well.

6 egg whites

350 g/1¾ cups caster/superfine sugar

150 ml/⅔ cup storebought raspberry coulis, for painting

baking sheets, lined with parchment paper

makes about 40

Preheat the oven to 110°C (215°F) Gas ½.

Pour water into a large saucepan until one third full and heat to simmering point over medium–low heat.

Put the egg whites and sugar in a wide, shallow metal bowl and lightly mix to combine. Sit the bowl over the pan of simmering water (making sure that the bottom of the bowl doesn't touch the water) and let the mixture heat up until it is warm to the touch and the sugar has dissolved. Stir occasionally.

Remove from the heat and whisk with an electric whisk until glossy and stiff peaks are reached.

Dot a bit of the mixture in each corner of the baking sheets and stick the parchment paper to it. Using 2 tablespoons, scoop the mixture into golf-ball sized meringues onto the prepared baking sheets.

Bake in the preheated oven for 50–60 minutes until firm. Remove the meringues from the oven. Using a pastry brush, paint raspberry coulis onto the meringues and put back into the oven to bake until the coulis has turned a darker, more purpley colour and the meringue is dry to the touch. The coulis can feel slightly sticky.

Remove from the oven and let cool. Remove from the parchment paper and store in an airtight container for up to 1 week.

VARIATIONS

PLAIN MERINGUES: add the seeds from ½ vanilla pod to the egg whites and sugar before heating.

OTHER FLAVOURS: dust cocoa powder or sprinkle crushed pistachios or desiccated coconut over the meringues just before baking.

foolproof vanilla macarons

There's a mystique that surrounds macarons, as if they are the realm of the French pastry chef. But broken down into their fundamental core – a crispy meringue-like shell filled with a soft cream – they're quite simple to achieve. To make those distinctive 'feet', you have to let the mixture sit for a bit before putting in the oven; it creates a skin which acts like a lid and forces the steam to come out from the edges, lifting the macaron off the tray and forming the feet. If you put the mixture immediately in the oven, the surface is flexible and instead will expand, much like a balloon, preventing the growth of feet. I got this recipe from Regis Cursan, the Regional Executive Pastry Chef at Nobu London. And yes, he's French.

macaron paste

300 g/2½ cups ground almonds

300 g/2¾ cups icing/confectioners' sugar

½ vanilla pod, seeds only

3 egg whites

Swiss meringue

300 g/1½ cups plus 2 tablespoons caster/superfine sugar

100 ml/½ cup water

3 egg whites

filling options

Fudge Icing (see page 88)

storebought dulce de leche (or to make your own, see page 136)

American Vanilla Buttercream (see page 86, plain or flavoured with rosewater)

Green Tea Pastry Cream (see page 83)

Milk Chocolate Sesame Cream (see page 75)

sugar thermometer

large piping bag fitted with a plain nozzle/tip

baking sheets lined with parchment paper

makes about 30

To make the macaron paste, put the ground almonds, icing/confectioners' sugar and vanilla seeds in a food processor and whiz until super-fine.

Transfer to a mixing bowl and fold in the egg whites until you get a paste. Let sit while you make the Swiss meringue.

To make the Swiss meringue, put the 300 g/1½ cups sugar and water in a medium saucepan and stir until combined. Bring to a boil, add a sugar thermometer and keep heating until the temperature on the thermometer reaches 110°C/230°F.

Meanwhile, put the egg whites and the remaining 2 tablespoons sugar in a large mixing bowl and start to whisk. When the sugar syrup in the pan reaches 110°C/230°F, whisk the egg whites to stiff peaks.

Slowly pour the hot sugar syrup into the egg whites and continue to whisk until stiff peaks are reached.

Take one third of the meringue and beat into the macaron paste to lighten. Gently fold in another third, then fold in the last third.

Fill the prepared piping bag with the mixture and pipe neat rounds about 4 cm/1½ inches across on the prepared baking sheets. Tap the baking sheets twice on the counter to flatten out the macaron mixture. Let sit for 30–45 minutes. Preheat the oven to 135°C (265°F) Gas 2.

Bake in the preheated oven for 10–12 minutes until you see feet form and the macarons look dry and dull on top.

Remove from the oven and let cool. When cold, remove from the parchment paper and sandwich with your filling of choice.

vanilla marshmallows

Marshmallows are a relatively new addition to our stores, and they were a special request from the lovely Elizabeth Hastrop, food buyer at Selfridges. Always on the lookout for the best food trends, we created a line of marshmallows especially for her. After a few tweaks to the standard marshmallow we added our own twist, by using golden syrup to really add a sense of depth to the marshmallow as well as provide stability to the sugar crystals. It's one of the most satisfying ways of enjoying flavour.

20 g/3 tablespoons powdered gelatine

120 ml/½ cup cold water

440 g/2¼ cups caster/superfine sugar

160 g/½ cup golden syrup

200 ml/¾ cup water

1 tablespoon vanilla extract

pan/cooking spray, for the baking pan

cornflour/cornstarch, for coating

sugar thermometer

brownie/baking pan, 30 x 20 x 5 cm/ 12 x 8 x 2 inches, lined with parchment paper

makes 24

Put the gelatine and the 120 ml/½ cup cold water in large mixing bowl and stir. Let sit and all the gelatine to swell or 'bloom'.

Put the sugar, golden syrup and the 200 ml/¾ cup water in a large saucepan and stir to combine. Brush the insides of the saucepan with clean water to dislodge any stray grains of sugar. Bring to a boil, add a sugar thermometer and keep cooking to bring to firm ball stage, 120°C/248°F.

Whisking furiously with an electric whisk (or in an electric mixer), slowly add the sugar syrup to the gelatine mixture. Whisk thoroughly until thick, bubble-gum-like strands form. Stir in the vanilla extract.

Spray everything with pan/cooking spray including spatulas, brownie pan, spoons, hands, etc. to avoid sticking!

Spoon the mixture into the prepared brownie pan and spread evenly. Sift some cornflour/cornstarch over the top and let rest for 2 hours.

Using a greased knife, cut the marshmallows into cubes and toss in cornflour/ cornstarch. Store in an airtight container for up to 2 weeks.

VARIATIONS

RASPBERRY: reduce the cold water to 60 ml/¼ cup for adding to gelatine. Fold in 60 ml/¼ cup storebought raspberry coulis until streaky. Continue recipe as above. After making and resting for 2 hours, tip the slab of marshmallow out of the pan onto a board, cut into squares and coat in 100 g/4 oz. ground, freeze-dried raspberries mixed with a little cornflour/cornstarch.

BAILEYS: replace the vanilla extract with a shot of Baileys (or more to taste).

sea salt caramels

I made these once on a lark. Then I put them in the store and they sold out in two days (covered in Valrhona chocolate). And then people came back week after week asking for them. Then they started a petition. Then I got carpal tunnel syndrome from cutting so many caramels. So now the caramels are only in the store periodically. I prefer not to dip them in chocolate, but it's really up to you.

175 g/½ cup golden syrup
100 ml/½ cup water
600 g/3 cups caster/superfine sugar
225 g/2 sticks unsalted butter
450 ml/1¾ cups whipping cream
Maldon sea salt, for sprinkling

sugar thermometer
brownie/baking pan, 30 x 25 x 5 cm/
    12 x 10 x 2 inches, oiled and lined
    with parchment paper

makes about 50

Put the golden syrup, water and sugar in a large, heavy-based saucepan and stir until well combined. Brush the insides of the saucepan with clean water to dislodge any stray grains of sugar.

Bring to a boil over high heat. When it reaches a boil, add the butter and cream. Let it come to a boil again, reduce the heat to medium–low heat and add a sugar thermometer.

Let the caramel reach 121°C/250°F, when it's near the end of the firm ball stage. If the caramel goes past 121°C/250°F you will have something more like toffee. If it is below, you'll have a caramel-fudgey sauce, but no confectionery. You might like to know that if something goes wrong, both outcomes are great as toppings on cupcakes!

Being very careful, pour the hot sugar syrup into the prepared brownie pan. Let set for 1 minute, than sprinkle sea salt all over the top. Be careful – the pan will be hot for a good while.

Let the caramel set for about 4–5 hours or overnight if it's a hot day.

Remove the caramel from the pan, peel off the paper and cut into desired shapes.

TIP: salt elevates and heightens the sweetness of these caramels. As there are hundreds of different varieties of salt, you can experiment, from the pink-hued *fleur de sel* from Brittany, to the finer granules of Cornish sea salt.

tarts

1 *2* *3* *4*

pâte brisée dough

It's always said that the recipe with the lowest number of ingredients tends to be the most difficult to execute. *Pâte brisée* is certainly one of those recipes. It's so easy to create a light, flaky crust that just bursts out of the pie tin. It's also so easy to make a rock-hard and shrunken shell that would be best used as a disposable plate. Pay attention to temperature, particularly keeping things as cold as possible, and don't worry about fully incorporating the butter, as it's better to underwork the dough than overwork it. Large streaks of butter when rolled out will laminate and create a quasi-puff-pastry effect.

280 g/2 cups plain/all-purpose flour

140 g/1¼ sticks unsalted butter, cut into 2-cm/¾-inch cubes and chilled

½ teaspoon salt

4 tablespoons ice-cold water

23-cm/9-inch tart pan/pie plate, greased

baking beans

makes enough for 2 × 23-cm/9-inch tarts

Put the flour, butter and salt in a large bowl and rub between your fingertips until a nice golden, sand-like texture emerges. Refrigerate for 15 minutes.

Add the ice-cold water and mix with a table knife until just combined. It should look sandy and clumpy. Cut the dough in half. Flatten each half lightly into a disc, wrap in clingfilm/plastic wrap and let sit for 10 minutes. You will only need one portion of dough, so freeze the other one for another time.

Preheat the oven to 170°C (340°F) Gas 5.

On a lightly floured surface, use a rolling pin to roll out the disc until 5 mm/⅛ inch thick. Roll the dough around the rolling pin and lift it over the prepared tart pan. Unroll it and smooth out the dough inside the pan. Roll the pin over the pan to trim off the excess dough around the edge. Refrigerate for about 10 minutes.

Line the pastry base with parchment paper and fill with baking beans. Blind-bake in the preheated oven for 20–25 minutes until dry and a light golden colour.

pâte sablée dough

Pâte sablée is characterized by the soft crumb that gives way when you bite into it. It's imperative that the butter and flour form a sandy consistency before you add any wet ingredients, hence the name *sablée*, from the French for 'sandy'. The same mechanics behind a perfect scone are also behind a great pie crust. Flakiness occurs because a butter molecule is surrounded by flour molecules. If kept in a cold state and put into a hot oven, the butter will instantly create steam, which creates tiny pockets of air, in turn creating the lovely flakiness we look for in a pie crust. Overworking the dough also creates gluten, which removes the flour molecules' role in coating the butter clumps, so no flakiness forms either. Treat the dough gently and it will reward you.

250 g/1¾ cups plain/all-purpose flour

120 g/1 stick unsalted butter, cut into 2-cm/¾-inch cubes and chilled

70 g/¾ cup icing/confectioners' sugar

2 eggs, lightly beaten

23-cm/9-inch tart pan/pie plate, greased

baking beans

makes enough for 2 x 23-cm/9-inch tarts

Put the flour and butter in a large bowl and rub between your fingertips until a nice golden, sand-like texture emerges. Refrigerate for 15 minutes.

Add the icing/confectioners' sugar and stir in. Add the eggs and knead lightly with your hands until it comes together into a smooth ball. The butter must be fully incorporated, but don't overknead it. Cut the dough in half. Flatten each half lightly into a disc, wrap in clingfilm/plastic wrap and let sit for 10 minutes. You will only need one portion of dough, so freeze the other one for another time.

Preheat the oven to 170°C (340°F) Gas 5.

On a lightly floured surface, use a rolling pin to roll out the disc until 5 mm/⅛ inch thick. Roll the dough around the rolling pin and lift it over the prepared tart pan. Unroll it and smooth out the dough inside the pan. Roll the pin over the pan to trim off the excess dough around the edge. Refrigerate for 10 minutes.

Line the pastry base with parchment paper and fill with baking beans. Blind-bake in the preheated oven for 20–25 minutes until dry and a light golden colour.

Key lime pie

This was the first pie I ever made and the recipe I used then was from *The Fannie Farmer Cookbook* by Marion Cunningham – a definitive American classic. This one is adapted from that original, which creates a sweet and tart baked milk custard, perfect for summertime.

400 g/14 oz. digestive biscuits/
graham crackers

75–100 g/¾–1 stick unsalted butter,
melted

1½ x 397-g/14-oz. cans of sweetened
condensed milk

freshly squeezed juice and grated zest
of 13 limes (no, really!)

8 egg yolks

a pinch of salt

vanilla whipped cream

400 ml/1⅔ cups double/heavy cream

40 g/⅓ cup icing/confectioners' sugar

1 teaspoon vanilla extract

*23-cm/9-inch pie dish/plate, greased
and lined with parchment paper*

baking beans

serves 8–10

Preheat the oven to 145°C (290°F) Gas 3.

To make the crust, crush the digestive biscuits/graham crackers until you get fine crumbs. Add the melted butter – the amount of butter you will need is variable. Test by grabbing a bit of the mixture and squeezing into your hand to make a ball, then releasing your hand. The mixture should hold its shape, but also fall apart when touched slightly. If it doesn't hold its shape, add more butter, otherwise the biscuit/cracker will dissolve into the cheesecake and you'll have no crust. If it holds its shape too well, add more biscuits/crackers to absorb the butter, otherwise your crust will be too hard.

Press the mixture into the pie dish/plate, going all the way up the side. Cover with a round of parchment paper and fill with baking beans to the top. Bake in the preheated oven for 12–20 minutes until the crust is firm and dry. Remove from the oven and let cool.

Adjust the oven temperature to 160°C (315°F) Gas 4.

To make the custard, whisk the condensed milk, lime juice and zest, egg yolks and salt together in a bowl and taste. If it is too tart, add a bit more condensed milk; not tart enough, add more lime juice. Pour into the baked pie shell and put back in the oven for 18–30 minutes until the top is set and the pie barely jiggles in the middle. (If it's poofy and cracked or brown on top, it's over.) Remove from the oven and let cool.

To make the vanilla whipped cream, combine all the ingredients in a bowl and whisk to stiff peaks. Spread over the pie and refrigerate for 2 hours before serving.

the ultimate coconut cream pie

I've always found archetypal coconut cream pies to fall short of my ideal – either they have a bland, pale pie crust, a too-sweet filling that doesn't taste of coconut or a watery meringue that seeps into the pie. So I thought, let's throw everything out the window and start again. This pie has a crumbly crust like a cheesecake, a super-coconutty pastry cream, a rich cream and Malibu topping and of course shredded coconut and drizzled chocolate on top. Heaven.

400 g/14 oz. HobNobs, graham crackers or anzac biscuits

75–100 g/¾–1 stick unsalted butter, melted

500 ml/2 cups double/heavy cream

50 g/½ cup icing/confectioners' sugar

½ teaspoon vanilla extract

1 shot of Malibu liqueur (or more)

Coconut Pastry Cream (page 83)

to decorate

soft shredded coconut e.g. Baker's Angel Flake (do not replace with desiccated coconut), toasted

dark/semi-sweet chocolate, melted

white chocolate, melted

23-cm/9-inch pie dish/plate, greased and baselined with parchment paper

baking beans

serves 8–10

Preheat the oven to 145°C (290°F) Gas 3.

To make the crust, crush the biscuits/graham crackers until you get fine crumbs. Add the melted butter – the amount of butter you will need is variable. Test by grabbing a bit of the mixture and squeezing into your hand to make a ball, then releasing your hand. The mixture should hold its shape, but also fall apart when touched slightly. If it doesn't hold its shape, add more butter, otherwise the biscuit/cracker will dissolve into the cheesecake and you'll have no crust. If it holds its shape too well, add more biscuits/crackers to absorb the butter, otherwise your crust will be too hard.

Press the mixture into the pie dish/plate, going all the way up the sides. Cover with a round of parchment paper and fill with baking beans to the top. Bake in the preheated oven for 12–20 minutes until the crust is firm and dry. Remove from the oven and let cool.

To make a Malibu whipped cream, combine the cream, icing/confectioners' sugar, vanilla extract and Malibu in a bowl and whisk to stiff peaks.

Spread a thin layer of the Malibu whipped cream over the base of the baked pie shell. Spoon the Coconut Pastry Cream into the pie and level with a spatula. Dollop the remaining Malibu whipped cream on top.

Sprinkle toasted flaked coconut over the top and drizzle with dark and white melted chocolate. Refrigerate for 1 hour before serving.

golden Bourbon pecan custard pie

To maximize the flavour of the Bourbon, it is brushed onto the warm pie. If you prefer, you can use another type of whisky. Vanilla ice cream is the best thing to eat with this, or better yet, a Bourbon-infused prune vanilla ice cream.

1 blind-baked Pâte Brisée pie crust
    (page 64)

Bourbon pecan custard

1 egg
2 egg yolks
250 g/⅔ cup golden syrup
150 g/¾ cup caster/superfine sugar
300 ml/1¼ cups double/heavy cream
¼ teaspoon freshly grated nutmeg
¼ teaspoon ground cardamom
1 teaspoon vanilla extract
250 g/2½ cups pecan halves
2 tablespoons Bourbon or any type
    of whisky you prefer

serves 8–10

Preheat the oven to 170°C (375°F) Gas 5.

To make the Bourbon pecan custard, put the egg and egg yolks in a large bowl and whisk together. Add the golden syrup and sugar and whisk thoroughly. Add the cream, nutmeg, cardamom and vanilla extract and whisk until combined.

Scatter the pecans evenly over the blind-baked pâte brisée pie crust. Pour the custard filling over the top.

Bake in the preheated oven for 30–40 minutes until the middle lightly jiggles but the rest is set.

Remove from the oven and place on a wire rack. While still warm, brush the Bourbon all over the top of the pie.

Let cool for 2 hours. Serve on the day of baking, or refrigerate for 1 day.

TIP: Bourbon is one of those classic American liqueurs that have wonderful buttery and molasses notes, which complement pecans beautifully. However, other whiskies can work just as well, or dark rum to add additional floral qualities.

poached pear & frangipane tart

This is one of those dessert classics that I just had to include in the book. Desert Island dilemma: you can only pick five desserts to stay with you (yes five – I can't pick just one). This would make the cut for me. The tart is showy – one of those desserts that make guests say 'wow' – particularly when paired with vanilla ice cream. In fact, for the tart you will only need four of the eight pears used, so keep the remaining poached pears in the fridge (for up to 1 week) and serve with vanilla ice cream for a no-fuss dessert.

1 blind-baked Pâte Sablée pie crust
(see page 65)

poached pears

1 bottle of Syrah or Merlot wine
700 ml/2¾ cups water
700 g/3½ cups caster/superfine sugar
grated zest of 1 orange
1 whole star anise
1 vanilla pod, split in half lengthways
2 cloves
3 cinnamon sticks, lightly crushed
4 cardamom pods, crushed
2 cm/1 inch fresh ginger, peeled
8 firm pears, e.g. Bosc or Williams

frangipane

250 g/2 sticks unsalted butter, softened
250 g/1¼ cups caster/superfine sugar
2 eggs
250 g/2 cups ground almonds
1 tablespoon cornflour/cornstarch

serves 8–10

To make the poached pears, put the wine, water, sugar, orange zest, anise, vanilla pod, cloves, cinnamon sticks, cardamom pods and ginger in a large saucepan. Cook over medium heat until reaching a nice simmer and all the sugar has dissolved.

Peel the pears. Add them, whole, to the poaching liquid and cover with a round of parchment paper. Place a plate on top of the paper to act as a weight, as pears like to float. Let simmer for 30 minutes over low heat.

When cooked, remove the pears from the poaching liquid (reserving the liquid) and let cool. Put 4 of the pears in the fridge to use at a later date.

Preheat the oven to 170°C (375°F) Gas 5.

Cut the remaining, cold pears into quarters and remove the core and stems. Slice the quarters into slim wedges and arrange over the base of the blind-baked pâte sablée pie crust.

To make the frangipane, put the butter and sugar in an electric mixer with paddle attachment (or use an electric whisk) and beat until lightened in colour and fluffy in texture. Gradually beat in the eggs, one at a time, until thoroughly combined.

Mix the cornflour/cornstarch and ground almonds in a separate bowl, then fold into the egg mixture until thoroughly combined.

Spoon the frangipane into the tart, all around the pear wedges. Bake in the preheated oven for 25–35 minutes until the filling is set and golden brown.

Remove from the oven and let cool.

Meanwhile, put 400 ml/1¾ cups of the reserved poaching liquid in a saucepan over medium–low heat and heat until it has reduced to a syrup-like consistency.

Glaze the cold tart with the poaching syrup and serve.

milk chocolate sesame cream tart with glazed cherries

I first learned about this milk chocolate sesame cream or 'cremoso' from my previous chef, Regis Cursan of Nobu. Of course, at the time, it was served with a Brazil-nut crumble biscuit, coconut sorbet, painted crushed sesame seeds, milk jelly and candied adzuki beans. I found myself wanting to eat this cream out of the bowl on its own. There is a more civilized way to eat it, hence this gooey tart. The sweet and sour cherries provide a nice counterpoint to the milk chocolate, and the sablée crust adds the perfect crunch.

1 blind-baked Pâte Sablée pie crust
   (see page 65)

milk chocolate sesame cream

4 egg yolks

350 ml/1½ cups whipping cream

150 ml/⅔ cup milk

400 g/14 oz. high-quality milk
   chocolate, chopped into pea-sized
   pieces

1 tablespoon good toasted sesame oil

glazed cherry topping

340-g/12-oz. jar of morello cherry
   preserve

80 ml/⅓ cup water

500 g/1 lb. good, sweet cherries,
   neatly pitted

500 g/1 lb. good, tart but edible
   cherries, neatly pitted

sugar thermometer

serves 8–10

To make the milk chocolate sesame cream, put the egg yolks in a large, heatproof bowl and whisk lightly.

Put the cream and milk in a saucepan over medium heat and heat up. Slowly pour them, in a steady stream, into the egg yolks, whisking continuously. When thoroughly combined, pour back into the saucepan and add a sugar thermometer.

Put the chocolate in a separate, large heatproof bowl.

Heat the egg mixture over low heat and stir continuously with a wooden spoon until the temperature on the thermometer reaches 75°C/167°F.

When the mixture reaches 75°C/167°F, pour it, through a strainer, into the bowl of milk chocolate. Stir until just combined.

Pour in the sesame oil and stir to combine. Pour into the blind-baked pâte sablée pie crust, then refrigerate for 3 hours.

To make the glazed cherry topping, put the cherry preserve and water in a small saucepan over medium heat and heat up until nice and hot, but not boiling.

Stir in the cherries and let cool slightly.

Pour the cherries and the glaze over the tart and serve immediately, or chilled.

green tea cream tart with strawberries & white chocolate

The green tea is the most important part of this tart, and the quality of the green tea (or matcha) determines the taste of the end result. Buying a lower-quality green tea will result in a bitter-tasting tart, but a lovely matcha will have grassy, sweet notes which pair perfectly with the strawberries and white chocolate. I humbly request that this dessert only be made during strawberry season; out-of-season strawberries will be too bland to stand up to the matcha.

Green Tea Pastry Cream (see page 83)

1 blind-baked Pâte Sablée pie crust (see page 65)

to decorate

2 punnets of ripe strawberries

70 g/2½ oz. strawberry jam

1 tablespoon water

white chocolate, melted, for drizzling

serves 8–10

Hull some of the strawberries and leave the prettiest stalks on the others.

Spoon the green tea pastry cream into the blind-baked pâte sablée pie crust and level with a spatula. Scatter the strawberries over the top in a decorative fashion, as you wish.

To decorate, put the strawberry jam and water in a small saucepan and bring to a boil, so that the jam is thin and hot. Brush or pour the glaze all over the strawberries, especially the cut tops, to make a glaze.

Drizzle melted white chocolate all over the strawberries to decorate.

Tip: if you wish to serve the tart a day in advance, brush the base of the blind-baked pie crust with melted white chocolate before adding the pastry cream, so that the crust doesn't get soggy while it sits in the fridge.

cake bases & fillings

lemon curd

This lemon curd is super-rich and tart. The method is also different from regular curds, as you actually cook it similarly to a *crème anglaise*, so it's much faster than by a *bain marie*. Keep in mind, though, that the risk of burning the mixture is higher, but such is life!

150 ml/⅔ cup freshly squeezed lemon juice (from approximately 5–6 unwaxed lemons), with the grated zest

125 g/⅔ cup caster/superfine sugar

8 egg yolks

125 g/1 stick plus 1 tablespoon unsalted butter, cubed

sugar thermometer

makes 600 g/1¼ lbs.

Put the lemon juice and zest and half the sugar in a large saucepan. Whisk until combined and cook over medium high heat until it reaches a boil.

When it has reached boiling point, in a large, heatproof bowl, whisk the egg yolks and remaining sugar. Slowly pour the hot lemon juice into the egg mixture, whisking quickly so as to avoid scrambling the eggs. Pour back into the pan, add a sugar thermometer and set over low heat. Whisk continuously until the temperature on the thermometer reaches 75°C/167°F.

Immediately remove from the heat and strain into another bowl. Whisk in the butter until melted and thoroughly combined. Lay a sheet of clingfilm/plastic wrap directly on the surface of the lemon curd, then let cool. Refrigerate for 1 hour before using. Store in an airtight container in the fridge for up to 1 week.

VARIATIONS

PASSIONFRUIT: replace the lemon juice with 160 ml/⅔ cup passionfruit juice or purée (available in the cocktail-making section of your local supermarket).

BLOOD ORANGE: replace the lemon juice and zest with the same quantities of blood orange juice and zest.

MANGO: keep the freshly squeezed juice of 1 lemon and replace the rest of the lemon juice and zest with 120 g/½ cup mango purée.

YUZU: replace the lemon juice with the same quantity of unsalted yuzu juice, or if you're lucky and can find it, the juice and zest of fresh or frozen yuzu.

vanilla pastry cream

This pastry cream is thicker than the typical English custard, making it suitable as a filling for cakes. The best thing about it is the use of cornflour/cornstarch, which allows for instant thickening and a neutral flavour. The traditional recipe for pastry cream requires at least 10 minutes of cooking the flour to activate it – any less and a floury, gluey taste could result, plus the eggs tend to overflavour the cream as well.

250 ml/1 cup milk
3 tablespoons caster/superfine sugar
2 egg yolks
2 teaspoons vanilla extract
1 tablespoon cornflour/cornstarch
35 g/2½ tablespoons unsalted butter

makes 375 g/13 oz.

Put the milk and half the sugar in a medium saucepan over medium heat and stir with a wooden spoon. Bring to a boil. As soon as it comes to a boil, remove from the heat and set aside.

Put the egg yolks in a large, heatproof bowl. In a separate bowl, combine the remaining sugar and the cornflour/cornstarch and mix thoroughly. Add to the egg yolks and vanilla extract and whisk thoroughly.

While the milk mixture is still hot, whisk it into the egg mixture in the bowl.

Strain the mixture back into the saucepan, set over medium–low heat and whisk continuously until it reaches a boil.

Strain the mixture again into a bowl and stir in the butter until melted and thoroughly combined. Lay a sheet of clingfilm/plastic wrap directly on the surface of the pastry cream, then let cool. Refrigerate for 30 minutes before using.

When ready to use, whisk lightly to bring back to a semi-soft consistency.

coconut pastry cream

Instead of using just coconut extracts like most other recipes, I thought, why not replace milk with coconut milk? The result is a super concentration of coconut flavour.

250 ml/1 cup coconut milk

50 ml/¼ cup coconut cream

3 tablespoons caster/superfine sugar

2 egg yolks

1 teaspoon vanilla extract

1 teaspoon coconut extract

2½ tablespoons cornflour/cornstarch

50 g/4 tablespoons unsalted butter

makes 450 g/1 lb.

Put the coconut milk and cream and half the sugar in a medium saucepan over medium heat and stir with a wooden spoon. Bring to a boil. As soon as it comes to a boil, remove from the heat and set aside.

Put the egg yolks, vanilla extract and coconut extract in a large, heatproof bowl. In a separate bowl, combine the remaining sugar and the cornflour/cornstarch and mix thoroughly. Add to the egg yolks and whisk thoroughly. While the milk mixture is still hot, whisk it into the egg mixture in the bowl. Strain the mixture back into the saucepan, set over medium–low heat and whisk continuously until it reaches a boil. Strain the mixture again into a bowl and stir in the butter until melted and thoroughly combined. Lay a sheet of clingfilm/plastic wrap directly on the surface of the pastry cream, then let cool. Refrigerate for 30 minutes before using.

When ready to use, whisk lightly to bring back to a semi-soft consistency.

green tea pastry cream

When shopping for green tea, look for matcha powder and not whole green tea leaves. Matcha powder is fragile, so keep it in the freezer when not in use.

4 teaspoons high-quality green tea powder (matcha powder)

250 ml/1 cup milk

60 g/⅓ cup caster/superfine sugar

2 egg yolks

½ teaspoon vanilla extract

1 tablespoon cornflour/cornstarch

35 g/2½ tablespoons unsalted butter

makes 375 g/13 oz.

Put the tea powder, milk and half the sugar in a medium saucepan over medium heat and stir with a wooden spoon. Bring to a simmering boil. As soon as it comes to a simmering boil, remove from the heat, cover and set aside.

Put the egg yolks and vanilla extract in a large, heatproof bowl. In a separate bowl, combine the remaining sugar and the cornflour/cornstarch and mix thoroughly. Add to the egg yolks and whisk thoroughly. While the milk mixture is still hot, whisk it into the egg mixture in the bowl. Strain the mixture back into the saucepan, set over medium–low heat and whisk continuously until it reaches a boil.

Strain the mixture again into a bowl and stir in the butter until melted and thoroughly combined. Lay a sheet of clingfilm/plastic wrap directly on the surface of the pastry cream, then let cool. Refrigerate for 30 minutes before using.

When ready to use, whisk lightly to bring back to a semi-soft consistency.

Italian buttercream

Buttercream is one of those great inventions of pastry – luscious, fluffy, silky and sweet. Again, temperature is key. The meringue needs to be cooled down enough to add the butter, otherwise the mixture will melt. If it does, put the mixture in the fridge for an hour and whip again when the butter has solidified. When adding flavourings, make sure they're at room temperature. If they're too cold, the buttercream won't incorporate the flavour thoroughly. A quick solution is to warm up some of the buttercream in the microwave to bring to room temperature.

360 g/1¾ cups caster/superfine sugar

1 tablespoon golden syrup

100 ml/½ cup water

6 egg whites

600 g/5 sticks unsalted butter, softened and cut into big chunks

flavouring of your choice: 3 teaspoons vanilla extract; 1 shot of espresso; melted chocolate; 1–2 shots of Baileys; freshly squeezed lemon juice and grated lemon zest; room-temperature raspberry coulis; slightly warmed peanut butter

sugar thermometer

makes 1 kg/2 lbs. or enough to frost 24 cupcakes

Put the sugar, golden syrup and water in a large saucepan and mix until well combined, making sure that no stray grains of sugar remain unmixed. Brush the inside of the saucepan with clean water to dislodge any stray grains. Set over high heat and bring to a rapid boil. When the sugar mixture has come to a boil, add a sugar thermometer and keep cooking until it reaches well into soft ball stage, 120°C/248°F. Remove from the heat.

Put the egg whites in a large, heatproof bowl if using an electric whisk (in which case you will need a second person to help you). Or use an electric mixer with whisk attachment. Whisk the egg whites to soft peaks.

Slowly pour a steady stream of sugar syrup into the egg whites, being careful not to hit the whisk while doing so. Continue whisking until the meringue cools slightly.

Add the softened butter one third at a time and whip until fully incorporated. Stir in the flavouring of your choice. Keeps for up to 1 week at room temperature.

American vanilla buttercream

There are four types of buttercream: Italian, which is an egg-white meringue enriched with butter (see page 84); Swiss, which is similar to Italian but the sugar isn't cooked and as a result doesn't cook the egg whites, so is highly perishable; French, which being French has to include egg yolks; and American, which isn't technically a buttercream at all but a frosting consisting of butter and icing sugar to replicate the qualities of real buttercream. American buttercream is essential to making archetypal American cupcakes. The milk helps to loosen up the buttercream when you don't want it to be too sweet. Think of sugar as a wet ingredient, so if the icing is still quite stiff but you don't want it to be sweeter, add milk to taste.

350 g/3 sticks unsalted butter, softened and cut into chunks

780 g/7 cups icing/confectioners' sugar

30–50 ml/2–3 tablespoons milk

1 tablespoon vanilla extract

makes enough to frost up to 24 cupcakes or to fill and cover a 20-cm/8-inch cake

Using an electric mixer with paddle or beater attachment (or an electric whisk), beat the butter and sugar until the mixture is lightened in colour and fluffy in texture. Stir in the milk and vanilla extract.

If it's not sweet enough, add more icing/confectioners' sugar. If it is too sweet but still stiff, add milk. If it is too sweet and really runny, add soft butter.

VARIATIONS

COCONUT: replace the milk with coconut milk and add 2 teaspoons coconut extract to boost the flavour.

RUM: replace the vanilla extract with dark rum.

MOCHA: add 2 tablespoons espresso and 3 tablespoons cocoa powder.

COOKIES & CREAM: add 200 g/6½ oz. lightly crushed Oreo cookies.

MINT: add 1 teaspoon mint extract and 1 teaspoon green food colouring.

fudge icing

The best showcase of chocolate is when it's paired with cream, either in mousse or truffle form – it's the ultimate expression of a chocoholic's dream. The key to this recipe is the addition of golden syrup to add elasticity and glossiness to the ganache. Pay attention to the stirring; the emulsion is tricky to make, but if you follow the recipe perfectly, you will be successful.

250 ml/1 cup whipping cream

65 g/3 tablespoons golden syrup

350 g/12 oz. high-quality dark/semi-sweet chocolate (we recommend Green & Blacks Organic 70%), chopped into pea-sized pieces

1 teaspoon vanilla extract

75 g/5 tablespoons unsalted butter, cut into cubes and chilled

makes enough to frost up to 24 cupcakes or to fill and cover a 20-cm/8-inch cake

Put the cream and golden syrup in a medium saucepan and bring to a boil.

Put the chocolate in a large, heatproof bowl. As soon as the cream mixture has come to a boil, immediately pour it over the chocolate. Set aside for 1 minute.

Using a small balloon whisk placed in the middle of the bowl, stir with very small motions. Don't stray from the middle of the bowl. You are making an emulsion by taking a large amount of chocolate at the bottom of the bowl and slowly adding small amounts of cream to it. Stirring in larger motions will incorporate more cream than needed, breaking the emulsion and resulting in a dull, grainy mixture. Do not incorporate air, as that will result in unwanted air bubbles and shorten the life of the icing. Keep stirring with small motions – it will look like nothing is happening until eventually a very shiny, thick, glossy mixture forms. Gradually stir in wider motions to incorporate more cream into the emulsion until it's fully combined.

Add the vanilla extract and butter and mix until well combined. Set aside to let the chocolate stiffen into a firm consistency before using.

cream cheese icing

I always make extra of this icing because it just tastes so good! It's used to fill the Gingerbread Guinness Cake on page 121 and ice the Hummingbird Cake on page 125. While cream cheese is thoroughly American, it tends to be full of stabilizers and fat (not that I'm complaining about the fat!). To lighten the icing, replace half the cream cheese with lebneh, a type of strained yogurt that can be easily found in Turkish and Middle Eastern supermarkets.

180 g/1½ sticks unsalted butter,
    softened
250 g/2¼ cups icing/confectioners'
    sugar
2 tablespoons golden syrup
800 g/1 lb. 12 oz. cream cheese
2 teaspoons vanilla extract

makes enough to frost up to 24 cupcakes or to fill and cover a 20-cm/8-inch cake

Using an electric mixer with paddle or beater attachment (or an electric whisk), beat the butter, sugar and golden syrup until the mixture is lightened in colour and fluffy in texture.

Add the cream cheese and vanilla extract and beat well.

VARIATIONS

MAPLE WALNUT CINNAMON: add an extra 3 tablespoons maple syrup, 1 teaspoon ground cinnamon and 100 g/¾ cup chopped walnuts.

CARDAMOM RUM: add 2 teaspoons ground cardamom, a pinch of freshly grated nutmeg and 3 tablespoons dark rum.

CHOCOLATE AMARETTO HAZELNUT: add 100 g/4 oz. melted dark/semi-sweet chocolate, 2 tablespoons Amaretto and 50 g/⅓ cup chopped hazelnuts.

the ultimate vanilla layer cake

This recipe is the definitive vanilla layer cake, as created by Shuna Lydon, one of the most talented pastry chefs in our generation. In it, temperature and method play the most important role in creating a light, buttery moist cake that plays well with anything you wish to pair it with, be it whipped cream and the best strawberry jam to make a Victoria sponge, fudge icing to make the classic American birthday cake or Italian buttercream to make a refined wedding cake. The beauty of the recipe is that it doesn't suffer from excess sugar – a common ploy by manufacturers to make a moist cake – but instead uses egg yolks and technique to create a lovely richness. This recipe was given to me by Shuna when she visited our kitchen and delighted us with other treats. I will be forever grateful for it.

200 g/1¾ sticks unsalted butter, softened

½ teaspoon salt

375 g/1¾ cups caster/superfine sugar

3 eggs, at room temperature

3 egg yolks, at room temperature

1 tablespoon vanilla extract

275 g/2 cups plain/all-purpose flour

2 teaspoons baking powder

160 ml/⅔ cup plus 1 tablespoon milk, lukewarm

icing/confectioners' sugar, for dusting

20-cm/8-inch round cake pan, greased and baselined with parchment paper

serves 8–12

Preheat the oven to 170˚C (340˚F) Gas 5.

Using an electric mixer with paddle or beater attachment (or an electric whisk), beat the butter, salt and sugar until the mixture is almost white in colour, fluffy in texture and the sugar has dissolved.

Slowly mix the whole eggs into the butter mixture, one at a time, beating until thoroughly combined before adding the next. Add the egg yolks, too, and mix well. Add the vanilla extract and mix.

In another bowl, combine the flour and baking powder well, so that the baking powder is thoroughly incorporated, and sift twice.

Add one third of the flour mixture to the egg mixture and mix until well incorporated. Add half the lukewarm milk and mix until just combined. Repeat with another third of the flour mixture, then the rest of the milk. Finally, add the last third of the flour mixture and mix until thoroughly combined.

Spoon the mixture into the prepared cake pan.

Bake in the preheated oven for 28–35 minutes. A wooden skewer inserted in the middle should come out with almost no crumbs attached, and the middle of the cake, when pressed, should spring back slightly instead of sink. Bake for an additional 5–10 minutes if necessary.

Remove from the oven and let cool in the pan for 10 minutes. Slide a table knife all around the edge to loosen the cake, then remove from the pan. Transfer to a wire rack to cool for 1 hour before cutting in half horizontally and filling with whipped cream and strawberry jam, Italian Buttercream (see page 84) or Fudge Icing (see page 88). Dust with icing/confectioners' sugar before serving.

the ultimate devil's food cake

It is imperative that natural cocoa powder and not Dutch-process cocoa powder be used in this recipe. Natural cocoa powder provides the acidity necessary to react with the baking soda, making it a moist and even crumb. The vegetable oil also helps to keep it moist, while the butter gives depth to the taste. This makes the most wonderful cupcake batter – super moist and even better the next day.

120 g/1 cup natural cocoa powder

250 ml/1 cup boiling water

125 ml/½ cup milk

1½ teaspoons vanilla extract

125 g/1 stick unsalted butter, softened

275 g/1⅓ cups dark brown soft sugar

165 g/¾ cup caster/superfine sugar

125 ml/½ cup vegetable oil

4 eggs

280 g/2 cups plain/all-purpose flour

1¼ teaspoons bicarbonate of/baking soda

muffin trays, lined with about 24 large cupcake cases, or 20-cm/8-inch round cake pan, greased and baselined with parchment paper

makes about 24 cupcakes or 1 cake serving 8–12

Preheat the oven to 170°C (340°F) Gas 5.

Put the cocoa powder in a bowl. Add the boiling water and mix well. Stir in the milk and vanilla extract and set aside.

Using an electric mixer with paddle or beater attachment (or an electric whisk), beat the butter and both sugars until the mixture is light in colour and fluffy in texture. Slowly pour in the oil in a steady stream and mix until combined. Add the eggs, one at a time, beating until thoroughly combined before adding the next. Scrape down the side of the bowl and mix again.

In another bowl, combine the flour and bicarbonate of/baking soda and sift twice.

Add one third of the flour mixture to the egg mixture and mix until well incorporated. Add half the cocoa/milk mixture and mix until just combined. Repeat with another third of the flour mixture, then the rest of the cocoa/milk mixture. Finally, add the last third of the flour mixture and mix until thoroughly combined.

Spoon the mixture into the cupcake cases or the prepared cake pan.

Bake in the preheated oven for 18–23 minutes for cupcakes, and 35–45 minutes for a cake. A wooden skewer inserted in the middle should come out with almost no crumbs attached, and the middle of the cake, when pressed, should spring back slightly instead of sink.

Remove from the oven and let cool in the muffin trays or cake pan for 10 minutes. If you've baked a cake, slide a table knife all around the edge to loosen it, then remove from the pan. Transfer to a wire rack to cool for 1 hour. Frost the cupcakes or the cake with fudge icing (see page 88) or frosting of your choice.

wheat-free Valrhona cake

This recipe is actually adapted from a lovely chocolate fondant recipe I learned at Nobu restaurant. Slightly tweaked, it becomes a wonderful wheat-free alternative with a great crumb and magnificent texture, something sorely lacking in most flourless cakes.

250 g/9 oz. Valrhona Araguani 72% Dark Chocolate, Scharffen Berger 70% or Green & Blacks Organic 70%, chopped into pea-sized pieces

250 g/2 sticks unsalted butter

5 eggs

2 egg yolks

100 g/½ cup caster/superfine sugar

30 g/3 tablespoons rice flour

30 g/3 tablespoons natural cocoa powder

20-cm/8-inch round cake pan, greased and baselined with parchment paper

serves 8–12

Preheat the oven to 170°C (340°F) Gas 5.

Put the chocolate in a large, heatproof bowl.

Melt the butter in a saucepan over high heat. Pour into the bowl of chocolate, stir until melted and smooth and set aside.

Using an electric mixer with whisk attachment (or an electric whisk), beat the eggs, egg yolks and sugar until pale and creamy in colour and quite thick – almost like a soft whipped cream.

Gently fold the egg mixture into the chocolate mixture.

Sift the rice flour and cocoa powder into the bowl and fold into the mixture.

Spoon the mixture into the prepared cake pan and bake in the preheated oven for 28–35 minutes. A wooden skewer inserted in the middle should come out with almost no crumbs attached, and the middle of the cake, when pressed, should spring back slightly instead of sink. Remove from the oven and let cool in the pan for 10 minutes. Slide a table knife all around the edge to loosen the cake, then remove from the pan. Transfer to a wire rack to cool for 1 hour.

vegan chocolate cake

It's vegan but we don't tell people it is and they love it. That's how good it is.

275 g/2 cups plain/all-purpose flour

100 g/¾ cup natural cocoa powder

2 teaspoons bicarbonate of/baking soda

1 teaspoon baking powder

a pinch of salt

450 ml/1¾ cups soya milk (e.g. Bonsoy or other unsweetened soya milk)

2 teaspoons red wine vinegar

320 g/1⅔ cups caster/superfine sugar

320 ml/1¼ cups sunflower oil

2 tablespoons vanilla extract

23-cm/9-inch round cake pan, greased and baselined with parchment paper

serves 8–12

Preheat the oven to 160°C (315°F) Gas 4.

Put the flour, cocoa powder, bicarbonate of/baking soda, baking powder and salt in a large mixing bowl. Sift twice.

In a separate bowl, whisk together the soya milk, vinegar, sugar, oil and vanilla extract. Pour into the flour mixture and stir until well combined.

Spoon the mixture into the prepared cake pan and bake in the preheated oven for 40–55 minutes. A wooden skewer inserted in the middle should come out with almost no crumbs attached, and the middle of the cake, when pressed, should spring back slightly instead of sink. Bake for an additional 5–10 minutes if necessary.

Remove from the oven and let cool in the pan for 10 minutes. Slide a table knife all around the edge to loosen the cake, then remove from the pan. Transfer to a wire rack to cool for 1 hour.

red velvet cake

The best food colouring we have found is Sugarflair's Red Extra paste, available online and from cake decorating stores. The icing for this ever-popular red velvet is very different from most other cream cheese icings because it's lightened with mascarpone and whipped cream. If you want a denser icing, merely omit the whipped cream.

2 eggs

225 g/1¼ cups caster/superfine sugar

1¼ teaspoons salt

250 ml/1 cup sunflower oil

1½ teaspoons vanilla extract

150 ml/⅔ cups buttermilk

2 teaspoons bicarbonate of/baking soda

2½ teaspoons apple cider vinegar or red wine vinegar

225 g/1⅓ cups plain/all-purpose flour

1½ tablespoons natural cocoa powder (or Dutch process if necessary)

¾ teaspoon red food colouring paste

ultimate cream cheese frosting

250 ml/1 cup whipping cream, very cold

175 g/¾ cup mascarpone

175 g/¾ cup cream cheese

85 g/¾ cup icing/confectioners' sugar, sifted

2 teaspoons vanilla extract

20-cm/8-inch round cake pan, greased and baselined with parchment paper

serves 8–12

Preheat the oven to 170°C (340°F) Gas 5.

Put the eggs, sugar and salt in a large mixing bowl and whisk together. While whisking, add the oil in a steady stream until fully combined and the mixture thickens slightly. Stir in the vanilla extract.

Put the buttermilk, bicarbonate of/baking soda and vinegar in a smaller, separate bowl. The mixture should bubble quite actively and then fade.

In another bowl, combine the flour and cocoa powder and sift twice.

Add one third of the flour mixture to the egg mixture and mix until well incorporated. Add half the buttermilk mixture and mix until just combined. Repeat with another third of the flour mixture, then the rest of the buttermilk. Finally, add the last third of the flour mixture and mix until thoroughly combined.

Add the food colouring last and stir until thoroughly incorporated. Spoon the mixture into the prepared cake pan.

Bake in the preheated oven for 28–35 minutes. A wooden skewer inserted in the middle should come out with almost no crumbs attached, and the middle of the cake, when pressed, should spring back slightly instead of sink. Bake for an additional 5–10 minutes if necessary.

To make the ultimate cream cheese frosting, whisk the whipping cream to stiff peaks. Set aside.

Put the mascarpone, cream cheese, icing/confectioners' sugar and vanilla extract in another bowl and beat until well combined.

Add one third of the whipped cream to the cream cheese mixture and beat until combined. Fold in the rest of the whipped cream until thoroughly combined. Refrigerate for about 15 minutes. Frosting must always be refrigerated, due to the fragility of whipped cream.

Cut the cake horizontally into 3 equal layers. Spread a little of the ultimate cream cheese frosting over one layer of cake and top with another layer. Spread a little more frosting over the second layer and top with the final layer. Spread the remaining frosting all over the cake using a spatula.

espresso Bourbon cake

This cake is earthiness defined. With the Bourbon, espresso and brown sugar, it has an undefinable richness that can't be resisted! The cake keeps quite well and moist as long as it's well wrapped.

225 g/2 sticks unsalted butter

4 shots of good espresso

110 g/1 cup natural cocoa powder

200 g/1 cup caster/superfine sugar

220 g/1 cup dark brown soft sugar

2 eggs

75 ml/¼ cup Bourbon

1 teaspoon vanilla extract

280 g/2 cups plain/all-purpose flour

1 teaspoon bicarbonate of/baking soda

½ teaspoon salt

20-cm/8-inch round cake pan, greased and baselined with parchment paper

serves 8–12

Preheat the oven to 170°C (340°F) Gas 5.

Put the butter in a large saucepan and melt, then stir in the espresso and cocoa powder. Add both sugars and the eggs and whisk thoroughly. Add 3 tablespoons of the Bourbon and the vanilla extract and set aside

Put the flour, bicarbonate of/baking soda and salt in a large mixing bowl and sift twice.

Slowly pour the espresso mixture into the flour mixture. (Tip: always mix wet ingredients into dry to prevent clumps of flour from forming.) Stir until well combined. The mixture should be very liquidy.

Spoon the mixture into the prepared cake pan.

Bake in the preheated oven for 28–35 minutes. A wooden skewer inserted in the middle should come out with almost no crumbs attached, and the middle of the cake, when pressed, should spring back slightly instead of sink. Bake for an additional 5–10 minutes if necessary.

Remove from the oven and let cool in the pan for 10 minutes. Slide a table knife all around the edge to loosen the cake, then remove from the pan. Transfer to a wire rack to cool for 1 hour. Brush the remaining Bourbon over the top before cutting in half horizontally and filling with frosting of your choice.

TIP: this Espresso Bourbon Cake can make a pleasing alternative for those who don't like fruit cake. It ages well, so just continually soak it in dark rum like you would a fruit cake and it will be heavenly.

chocolate buttermilk cake

This was the chocolate cake recipe I first learned in a professional kitchen at Renee's and I have found no other recipe to better it. It has all the qualities you want in a chocolate layer cake – the chocolate mouthfeel, a buttery aftertaste, a fine, feathery crumb and a perfect density to stand up to any type of filling. I have searched far and wide to find a recipe similar to this, that uses chocolate, cocoa powder, buttermilk and obscene amounts of butter, but this is the only one. In my opinion it's the ultimate. I'm surprised Renee let me print it!

225 g/8 oz. high-quality dark/semi-sweet chocolate (we recommend Green & Blacks Organic 70%), chopped into pea-sized pieces

65 g/4 tablespoons Dutch-process cocoa powder

175 g/1½ sticks unsalted butter

4 eggs

300 g/1½ cups caster/superfine sugar

175 g/1¼ cups plain/all-purpose flour

½ teaspoon bicarbonate of/baking soda

¼ teaspoon salt

235 ml/1 cup buttermilk

1 x 25-cm/10-inch or 2 x 18-cm/7-inch cake pans, greased and baselined with parchment paper

serves about 20

Preheat the oven to 170°C (340°F) Gas 5.

Put the chocolate and cocoa powder in a large, heatproof bowl.

Melt the butter in a saucepan over medium–high heat. Pour into the bowl of chocolate and cocoa and stir until melted and smooth.

In another bowl, whisk together the eggs and sugar. Pour into the chocolate mixture and mix until well combined.

Put the flour, bicarbonate of/baking soda and salt in a large mixing bowl and sift twice.

Add one third of the flour mixture to the chocolate mixture and mix until well incorporated. Add half the buttermilk and mix until just combined. Repeat with another third of the flour mixture, then the rest of the buttermilk. Finally, add the last third of the flour mixture and mix until thoroughly combined.

Spoon the mixture into the prepared cake pan.

Bake in the preheated oven for 35–45 minutes. A wooden skewer inserted in the middle should come out with almost no crumbs attached, and the middle of the cake, when pressed, should spring back slightly instead of sink. Bake for an additional 5–10 minutes if necessary.

Remove from the oven and let cool in the pan for 10 minutes. Slide a table knife all around the edge to loosen the cake, then remove from the pan. Transfer to a wire rack to cool for 1 hour. Cut in half horizontally and fill with frosting of your choice.

almond frangipane cake

This requires almond paste, which provides a super-smooth consistency. Look for almond paste with a maximum of 50% sugar content plus just almonds (or marzipan if it's 50–60% almonds plus sugar). Lower-quality marzipan contains too much sugar, resulting in an uncake-like brick.

250 g/2 sticks unsalted butter, softened

5 tablespoons caster/superfine sugar

600 g/1 lb. 5 oz. almond paste (e.g. from King Arthur Flour or Anthon Berg Raa Marzipan, 60% almonds)

6 eggs

280 g/2 cups plain/all-purpose flour

1½ tablespoons baking powder

1 x 25-cm/10-inch or 2 x 18-cm/7-inch cake pans, greased and baselined with parchment paper

serves about 20

Preheat the oven to 160°C (315°F) Gas 4.

Using an electric mixer with paddle or beater attachment (or an electric whisk), beat the butter, sugar and almond paste until well combined. Slowly mix the eggs into the butter mixture, one at a time, until thoroughly combined and fluffy. Now beat for an additional 2 minutes.

Put the flour and baking powder in a large mixing bowl and sift twice. Fold into the almond mixture. Spoon the mixture into the prepared cake pan and bake in the preheated oven for 35–45 minutes. A wooden skewer inserted in the middle should come out with almost no crumbs attached. Bake for an additional 5–10 minutes if necessary. Remove from the oven and let cool in the pan for 10 minutes. Slide a table knife all around the edge to loosen the cake, then remove from the pan. Transfer to a wire rack to cool for 1 hour.

almond tea cake

I love me a pound cake, but one of the things that bugs me about it is that it can be cloyingly sweet, and sometimes sit in your stomach like a heavy lump. The solution? Ground almonds to provide structure and lighten the cake, and yogurt to help lessen the dependency on sugar and also to provide acidity to lighten the crumb as well. This is the kind of cake where you have one slice, then another an hour later and by the end of the day you'll wonder where it all went.

240 g/1 cup plus 2 tablespoons
 caster/superfine sugar

grated zest of 1 unwaxed lemon

150 g/1 cup plus 1 tablespoon plain/
 all-purpose flour

70 g/½ cup ground almonds

2 teaspoons baking powder

a pinch of salt

130 g/½ cup Greek yogurt

3 eggs

½ teaspoon vanilla extract

¼ teaspoon almond extract

80 ml/⅓ cup sunflower oil

50 g/3 tablespoons unsalted butter,
 melted

*20-cm/8-inch round cake pan, greased
 and baselined with parchment
 paper*

serves 8–12

Preheat the oven to 170°C (340°F) Gas 5.

Put the sugar and lemon zest in a large mixing bowl and rub with your hands until it smells lemony. Add the flour, almonds, baking powder and salt and mix well.

Put the yogurt, eggs and vanilla and almond extracts in a separate bowl and whisk until thoroughly combined. Add to the dry mixture and mix until just combined and no trace of dry flour remains. Fold in the oil and melted butter. Spoon the mixture into the prepared cake pan and bake in the preheated oven for 28–35 minutes. A wooden skewer inserted in the middle should come out with almost no crumbs attached. Bake for an additional 5–10 minutes if necessary. Remove from the oven and let cool in the pan for 10 minutes. Slide a table knife around the edge to loosen the cake, then remove from the pan. Transfer to a wire rack to cool for 1 hour.

apple Bourbon pecan cake

This easily makes my Desert Island top five – it's moist, it's packed with fruit and flavour and it has the type of flavouring that reminds you of the holidays. It's the kind of cake you smuggle into the cinema. You'll make furtive glances while you chow down and your neighbouring movie-goers will want to know where that heavenly smell is coming from. Not that I've ever done anything like that before.

225 g/2 sticks unsalted butter, softened

220 g/1 cup plus 1 tablespoon caster/superfine sugar

220 g/1 cup plus 1 tablespoon dark brown soft sugar

3 eggs

280 g/2 cups plain/all-purpose flour

1 teaspoon baking powder

½ teaspoon bicarbonate of/baking soda

1 teaspoon ground allspice

1½ teaspoons ground cinnamon

1 teaspoon freshly grated nutmeg

¼ teaspoon ground cloves

¼ teaspoon ground ginger

¼ teaspoon ground cardamom

½ teaspoon salt

3 tablespoons Bourbon

3 Granny Smith apples, peeled, cored and cut into chunks

120 g/1 cup shelled whole pecans, toasted and roughly chopped

20-cm/8-inch round cake pan, greased and baselined with parchment paper

serves 8–12

Preheat the oven to 160°C (315°F) Gas 4.

Using an electric mixer with paddle or beater attachment (or an electric whisk), beat the butter and both sugars until the mixture is almost light in colour and fluffy in texture.

Add the eggs, one at a time, beating until thoroughly combined before adding the next. Scrape down the side of the bowl and mix again for 1 minute.

In another bowl, combine the flour, baking powder, bicarbonate of/baking soda, all the spices and salt and sift twice.

Add one third of the flour mixture to the egg mixture and mix until well incorporated. Repeat with another third of the flour mixture, then the rest of the flour mixture and mix until just combined.

Pour the Bourbon over the apples in a bowl and mix. Fold the apples and pecans into the cake mixture.

Spoon the mixture into the prepared cake pan.

Bake in the preheated oven for 55–70 minutes. A wooden skewer inserted in the middle should come out with almost no crumbs attached, and the middle of the cake, when pressed, should spring back slightly instead of sink. Bake for an additional 5–10 minutes if necessary.

Remove from the oven and let cool in the pan for 10 minutes. Slide a table knife all around the edge to loosen the cake, then remove from the pan. Transfer to a wire rack to cool for 1 hour.

leftovers trifle

You are bound to have leftovers of everything around when you're baking, particularly when you're in a cake-baking frenzy! Here's what to do with all the leftovers, creating a multi-coloured fantasy trifle, complete with strawberries and Grand Marnier, which work so well with both chocolate and vanilla. The tops of any cake freeze really well, so after you make and assemble a cake, take the scraps that you've cut off the cake and freeze for up to a month. Dedicated bakers should be able to have enough to make this trifle in 3 weeks – or, if in a baking frenzy, one day!

off-cuts of The Ultimate Vanilla Layer Cake (see page 91), Red Velvet Cake (see page 97), Chocolate Buttermilk Cake (see page 101) or any combination!

Grand Marnier, for brushing

Vanilla Pastry Cream (see page 82)

2 punnets of ripe strawberries, hulled and quartered

Ultimate Cream Cheese Frosting (see page 97)

strawberry jam

small round cutters (optional)

large trifle dish

serves few or many!

If you like, cut the off-cuts of cake into neat rounds with small cutters and set aside. Reserve any remaining off-cuts. Brush all the pieces with Grand Marnier.

In the bottom of the trifle dish, spoon about half the vanilla pastry cream in an even layer, then about half the strawberries, then about one third of the ultimate cream cheese frosting in a neat layer, then all the strawberry jam.

Arrange a layer of the cake off-cuts over the strawberry jam, and place the neat rounds of cake upright all around the edge of the dish. Top with a layer of the remaining pastry cream and luscious spoonfuls of the remaining ultimate cream cheese frosting. Top with the remaining strawberries.

VARIATIONS

TROPICAL LEFTOVERS TRIFLE: to the same off-cuts of cake above, add Coconut Pastry Cream (see page 83), sliced mangoes, Malibu, Passionfruit Curd (see page 81) and white chocolate shavings.

CHOCOLATE RUM TRIFLE: to off-cuts of Red Velvet Cake and Chocolate Buttermilk Cake, add Vanilla Pastry Cream (see page 82), dark rum, Fudge Icing (see page 88), raspberry jam and raspberries.

special cakes

the Renee

When I first encountered this cake during my apprenticeship it was actually called La Victoria, with perfectly piped columns of meringue framing the outside. My first attempt looked as if the Michelin man mascot had undergone radioactive meltdown. As there is already a Victoria sponge in the UK I have renamed the cake 'The Renee' in honour of its creator, Renee Senne. It's light, creamy and the perfect summer birthday celebration cake.

The Ultimate Vanilla Layer Cake (see page 91)

50 ml/3 tablespoons Framboise liqueur

a small amount of Vanilla Pastry Cream (see page 82)

2 punnets of raspberries

Italian meringue frosting

360 g/1¾ cups caster/superfine sugar

1 tablespoon golden syrup

100 ml/½ cup water

6 egg whites

sugar thermometer
cook's blowtorch

serves 8-12

To make the Italian meringue frosting, put the sugar, golden syrup and water in a large saucepan and mix until well combined, making sure that no stray grains of sugar remain unmixed. Brush the inside of the saucepan with clean water to dislodge any stray grains. Set over high heat and bring to a rapid boil.

While the sugar mixture is heating, put the egg whites in a large, heatproof bowl if using an electric whisk (in which case you will need a second person to help you). Or use an electric mixer with whisk attachment. Whisk the egg whites to soft peaks.

When the sugar mixture has come to a boil, add a sugar thermometer and keep cooking until it reaches well into soft ball stage, 115°C/240°F. Remove from the heat. Slowly pour a steady stream of sugar syrup into the egg whites, being careful not to hit the whisk while doing so. Continue whisking until the meringue cools slightly.

Cut The Ultimate Vanilla Layer Cake horizontally into 3 equal layers.

Put one layer on a cake stand or plate. Brush with one third of the Framboise liqueur. Add a good smear of Vanilla Pastry Cream and spread evenly up to 1 cm/ ½ inch away from the edge of the cake. Dot with half the raspberries.

Repeat this process with a second layer of cake on top of the first layer. Top with the last layer. Brush with the remaining Framboise liqueur.

Take a spatula (or a piping bag) and decorate the cake all over with the Italian meringue frosting. Brown the frosting lightly with a cook's blowtorch.

vanilla coconut cake with lemon curd & cheesecake filling

If you have a friend or relative who hates chocolate and hates fruit, we've found this one to be a good compromise without being all vanilla. It's light, refreshing, stays moist, and is a good bake-ahead cake for those special occasions.

The Ultimate Vanilla Layer Cake
(see page 91)

vanilla-flavoured Italian Buttercream
(see page 84)

a small amount of Lemon Curd (see page 81)

125 g/4½ oz. toasted coconut chips

vanilla cheesecake filling

200 g/7 oz. cream cheese

60 g/⅓ cup caster/superfine sugar

1 small egg, lightly beaten

1 tablespoon cornflour/cornstarch

60 ml/¼ cup whipping cream

a couple of drops of vanilla extract

20-cm/8-inch round loose-bottomed cake pan, greased and baselined with parchment paper

piping bag fitted with a 1-cm/½-inch nozzle/tip

serves 8-12

Preheat the oven to 130°C (275°C) Gas 1.

To make the vanilla cheesecake filling, put the cream cheese and sugar in a bowl and beat until well mixed and the sugar has dissolved.

Slowly incorporate the egg, mixing very well before adding more. Sift the cornflour/cornstarch into the mixture and stir until thoroughly combined.

Add the cream and vanilla extract and mix until combined. Pour the mixture into the prepared baking pan and bake in the preheated oven for 15–20 minutes.

Remove from the oven and let cool until cold.

When you are ready to assemble the cake, cut The Ultimate Vanilla Layer Cake horizontally into 2 equal layers.

Put one layer on a cake stand or plate. Spread a very thin layer of vanilla-flavoured Italian Buttercream over the cake.

Put a few spoons of the buttercream into the prepared piping bag. Pipe a circular border of buttercream around the cake no closer than 1 cm/½ inch from the edge. This will act as a flooding wall to keep the lemon curd from seeping out.

Fill the inside of the border with a thin layer of lemon curd – but no higher than two thirds of the way up the buttercream, otherwise the lemon curd will seep out.

Very gently remove the cold cheesecake from the cake pan. Lay it carefully on top of the cake. Refrigerate for 30 minutes to allow the buttercream to set.

Pipe another border of buttercream, as described above, on top of the cheesecake and fill with lemon curd again. Place the remaining layer of cake on top and refrigerate for 20 minutes.

Spread the rest of the buttercream all over the cake with a spatula and coat with the flaked coconut.

triple chocolate cake

Every single chocoholic couple who has come in for a wedding cake tasting, picks this cake for their own. Layers of dense chocolate cake, chocolate buttercream and fudge icing are a chocoholic's dream. The buttermilk cake base holds particularly well for wedding cake decorating, and can hold syruping well if you need it. And by syruping I mean dousing with copious amounts of rum, or Bourbon, or brandy, or whisky…

70 g/2½ oz. dark/semi-sweet chocolate, roughly chopped
Italian Buttercream (see page 84, but follow the method opposite)
Chocolate Buttermilk Cake (see page 101)
Fudge Icing (see page 88)
honeycomb/sponge candy or other candy bars, roughly chopped, to decorate

serves about 20

To make a chocolate meringue buttercream, put the chocolate in a large heatproof bowl over a saucepan of simmering water. Do not let the base of the bowl touch the water. Leave until the chocolate has melted, then stir with a wooden spoon until smooth. Remove from the heat and let cool to room temperature.

Whisk the cooled, melted chocolate into the Italian Buttercream until thoroughly combined.

Cut the Chocolate Buttermilk Cake horizontally into 3 equal layers.

Put one layer on a cake stand or plate. Spread a thin layer of Fudge Icing over it. Now spread a generous layer of the chocolate meringue buttercream over the top.

Repeat this process with a second layer of cake on top of the first layer. Top with the last layer. Spread a thin layer of chocolate meringue buttercream all over the cake with a spatula, making it as smooth and neat as possible. Refrigerate for 1 hour.

A few minutes before you are ready to take the cake out of the fridge to finish decorating, you will need to soften the remaining fudge icing so that it's a pourable consistency. Be careful because it's an emulsion, so it's prone to splitting. Gently warm the icing in a microwave (or in a heatproof bowl over a saucepan of simmering water) for 10 seconds at a time. Keep checking and warming until it is smooth, runny and glossy. Take the cake out of the fridge and carefully pour the icing over it. Let cool and set slightly before decorating with chopped honeycomb/sponge candy or other candy bars.

frangipane raspberry cake

While hard at work apprenticing under Renee, my tasks consisted of washing pots and pans, sweeping and mopping the floor, deseeding raspberry jam and the like. When the time for my first birthday there rolled around, Renee asked what kind of cake I would like. Out of all the delectable choices possible, I picked this cake. The super-moist crumb, tart raspberry jam and smooth buttercream made it the ultimate birthday cake. As my first birthday cake during my pastry career, it's one I'll never forget.

Almond Frangipane Cake (see page 102)

vanilla-flavoured Italian Buttercream (see page 84)

1 jar of organic raspberry jam (I always like to use organic jam because I find it has a lower sugar content than most – don't settle for less than 55% fruit content)

2–3 punnets of raspberries

large piping bag fitted with St. Honoré nozzle/tip

serves about 20

Cut the Almond Frangipane Cake horizontally into 3 equal layers.

Put one layer on a cake stand or plate. Spread a very thin layer of vanilla-flavoured Italian Buttercream over the cake.

Put a few spoons of the buttercream into the prepared piping bag. Pipe a circular border of buttercream around the cake no closer than 1 cm/½ inch from the edge. This will act as a flooding wall to keep the raspberry jam from seeping out.

Fill the inside of the border with a thin layer of raspberry jam – but no higher than two thirds of the way up the buttercream, otherwise the jam will seep out. Place the second layer of cake on top and refrigerate for 20 minutes to allow the buttercream to set.

Pipe another border of buttercream, as described above, on top of the cake and fill with raspberry jam again. Place the remaining layer of cake on top and refrigerate for 20 minutes.

Spread a thin layer of the buttercream all over the cake.

Fill the prepared piping bag with the buttercream and, starting from the bottom of the cake, pipe feathers up the side of the cake in one fluid motion. Let the feathers go above the height of the cake if needed. Practise on a plate first, if you like!

Top with a mound of raspberries.

espresso Bourbon cake with mocha buttercream

This cake is a coffee fanatic's dream. So much so that I don't know if you'd want to even drink it with a coffee, as you could go into overload. But I'd be willing to try it anyway, wouldn't you? The cake keeps for 3 days on the kitchen counter under a cake dome, so it's the perfect cake to just have lying around the house when you're in the mood for a treat.

Espresso Bourbon Cake (see page 98)
Mocha American Buttercream (see page 86)
whole coffee beans

large piping bag fitted with a star-shaped nozzle/tip

serves 8–12

Cut the Espresso Bourbon Cake horizontally into 3 equal layers.

Put one layer on a cake stand or plate. Spread a thick layer of Mocha American Buttercream over the cake.

Repeat this process with a second layer of cake on top of the first layer. Top with the last layer.

Fill the prepared piping bag with the buttercream and pipe rosettes all around the edge of the cake. Decorate each rosette with a whole coffee bean.

TIP: elevate this cake by using super high-quality espresso. We use Square Mile coffee beans, and as we don't have super-fancy espresso machines at home, the wonderful AeroPress creates an ultra-concentrated shot of espresso that's perfect for the mocha buttercream needed in this recipe.

gingerbread Guinness cake with poached pears & cream cheese icing

This fabulous creation makes the perfect festive treat for those who may have overdosed on traditional Christmas cakes and desserts. The cake is redolent with Christmas spices, but the red-wine poached pears and cream cheese icing add a refreshing quality that makes it possible to enjoy a very hearty slice. Or two. Or three. This cake is quite spicy and strong, which means it can also pair up well with Fudge Icing (see page 88) and transform it from something refreshing to a super-dense, velvety treat. We had a chocolate version in the shop once, and when I had a wedding cake consultation, the groom took one taste of it and proclaimed: 'Done! That's the winner.'

Gingerbread Guinness Cupcakes (see page 44, but make the recipe in a 25-cm/10-inch cake pan as described in the Variation)

Cream Cheese Icing (see page 89)

1 batch of poached pears, sliced into wedges (from the Poached Pear and Frangipane Tart recipe on page 72)

½ small jar of apricot jam

chunks of crystallized ginger

serves about 20

Cut the Gingerbread Guinness Cake horizontally into 3 equal layers.

Put one layer on a cake stand or plate. Spread a thick layer of Cream Cheese Icing over the cake in generous dollops. Arrange some wedges of poached pear on top of the icing.

Repeat this process with a second layer of cake on top of the first layer. Top with the last layer.

Arrange more wedges of poached pear artfully on top of the cake.

Warm the apricot jam in a small saucepan over gentle heat and strain. Pour it over the pears on top of the cake. Decorate with chunks of crystallized ginger.

vegan chocolate mousse cake with fresh berries

Most vegan-style cakes tend to use all sorts of stabilizers and artificial chemicals to emulate cream and butter in a recipe. I say, why do you need to when chocolate has plenty of cocoa butter on its own to create a lovely mousse? The recipe is tricky and requires a bit of practice to get right. But once you get a feel for it, it'll be the easiest thing to make. And the tastiest, too.

1 Vegan Chocolate Cake (see page 95)
2 punnets of raspberries
2 punnets of strawberries, hulled and quartered
handful of crystallized violets

vegan chocolate mousse

800 g/1 lb. 12 oz. high-quality dark/semi-sweet chocolate, chopped into pea-sized pieces
600 ml/2½ cups hot water
you will also need lots of ice

serves 8–12

To make the vegan chocolate mousse, put the chocolate in a very large, wide heatproof bowl over a saucepan of simmering water (do not let the base of the bowl touch the water). Leave until melted, then stir with a wooden spoon until smooth and glossy.

Pour the hot water into the bowl of chocolate and mix until nice and smooth.

Sit the bowl in a dish filled with ice cubes. Using an electric whisk, quickly whisk the chocolate and water mixture thoroughly and quickly until a stiff mousse forms. If the mousse is too stiff, add a tiny bit of warm water, or better yet, some rum or espresso. If the mousse is too loose, add some more melted chocolate and quickly whisk up again.

Cut the Vegan Chocolate Cake horizontally into 3 layers.

Put one layer on a cake stand or plate. Spread one third of the vegan chocolate mousse over the cake in generous dollops. Arrange raspberries and strawberries over the top.

Repeat this process with a second layer of cake on top of the first layer. Top with the last layer.

Spread the remaining vegan chocolate mousse over the top of the cake and decorate with the remaining berries (or just raspberries) and crystallized violets.

hummingbird cake

Hummingbird cake is one of those classic Southern confections where you combine the most incongruous tropical items – pineapple, coconut and bananas – and create a homey American classic. We give it an additional flair with cardamom and rum to make it just a touch more tropical. Also, I must note that I normally loathe using pineapple pieces in light syrup, but it needs that sugar push to make it a proper hummingbird cake.

3 eggs

300 g/1½ cups caster/superfine sugar

140 g/⅔ cup light brown soft sugar

250 ml/1 cup sunflower oil

425 g/3 cups plain/all-purpose flour

½ teaspoon freshly grated nutmeg

¼ teaspoon ground allspice

1 teaspoon ground cinnamon

½ teaspoon ground cardamom

1 teaspoon bicarbonate of/baking soda

250 g/9 oz. chopped banana (from about 3–4 bananas)

225 g/8 oz. canned pineapple pieces in light syrup, drained well

100 g/1 cup soft shredded coconut e.g. Baker's Angel Flake (do not replace with desiccated coconut)

100 g/¾ cup shelled pecans, crushed, plus about 150 g/1 cup, crushed, to decorate

1 tablespoon dark rum

Cream Cheese Icing (see page 89)

23-cm/9-inch round cake pan, greased and baselined with parchment paper

serves 8–12

Preheat the oven to 160°C (315°F) Gas 4.

Using an electric mixer with paddle or beater attachment (or an electric whisk), whisk the eggs and both sugars together. While whisking, add the oil in a steady stream until fully combined.

In another bowl, combine the flour, all the spices and the bicarbonate of/baking soda and sift twice.

Add the flour mixture to the egg mixture and mix slowly until just combined. Add the bananas, pineapple pieces, coconut and pecans and mix until well combined. Stir in the rum.

Spoon the mixture into the prepared cake pan.

Bake in the preheated oven for 50–60 minutes. A wooden skewer inserted in the middle should come out with almost no crumbs attached, and the middle of the cake, when pressed, should spring back slightly instead of sink. Bake for an additional 5–10 minutes if necessary.

Remove from the oven and let cool in the pan for 10 minutes. Slide a table knife all around the edge to loosen the cake, then remove from the pan. Transfer to a wire rack to cool for 1 hour.

Cut the cooled cake horizontally into 2 equal layers, but be careful, as the pineapple and pecans can tear the cake. Put one cake layer on a cake stand or plate. Spread a layer of Cream Cheese Icing over the cake. Place the remaining layer of cake on top and spread the rest of the icing all over the cake with a spatula.

Cover the bottom half of the outside of the cake with crushed pecans.

cheesecakes

vanilla cheesecake with berries

New-York style cheesecakes are typically baked in a hot oven to begin with and then the oven is turned off, helping to create a dark brown crust and a soft, silky texture. Other cheesecake recipes require high heat and a water bath to gently cook the cheesecake; however, the top of a cheesecake is still exposed to hot air and thus prone to cracking. We wanted a compromise, a gently cooked cheesecake, and what better way to achieve that than with low heat all the way through? No muss or fuss with water baths and loose-bottomed cake pans.

400 g/14 oz. digestive biscuits/
   graham crackers

75–100 g/¾–1 stick unsalted butter,
   melted

800 g/1 lb. 12 oz. cream cheese

225 g/1 cup plus 1 tablespoon caster/
   superfine sugar

2 eggs

50 g/½ cup plus 1 tablespoon
   cornflour/cornstarch

250 ml/1 cup whipping cream

1 teaspoon vanilla extract

topping

250 ml/1 cup whipping cream

250 g/1 cup mascarpone

60 g/½ cup icing/confectioners' sugar,
   plus extra for dusting

1 tablespoon vanilla extract

1 punnet of raspberries

1 punnet of strawberries, hulled and
   halved

1 punnet of blackberries

1 punnet of blueberries

*25-cm/10-inch cake pan, greased and
   baselined with parchment paper*

serves 10–12

Preheat the oven to 125°C (240°F) Gas 1.

To make the crust, crush the digestive biscuits/graham crackers until you get fine crumbs. Add the melted butter – the amount of butter you will need is variable. Test by grabbing a bit of the mixture and squeezing into your hand to make a ball, then releasing your hand. The mixture should hold its shape, but also fall apart when touched slightly. If it doesn't hold its shape, add more butter, otherwise the biscuit/cracker will dissolve into the cheesecake and you'll have no crust. If it holds its shape too well, add more biscuits/crackers to absorb the butter, otherwise your crust will be too hard.

Press the mixture into the prepared cake pan and pat down until level.

Put the cream cheese and sugar in a bowl and beat until well mixed and the sugar has dissolved.

Slowly incorporate the eggs, one at a time, beating until thoroughly combined before adding the next. Scrape the side of the bowl regularly to make sure everything is incorporated.

Sift the cornflour/cornstarch into the mixture and stir until thoroughly combined. Add the cream and vanilla extract and mix until combined. Pour the mixture into the cake pan over the crust and bake in the preheated oven for 1 hour 20 minutes until the middle is slightly jiggly and the top doesn't look shiny or wet any more.

Remove from the oven and let cool in the pan for 1 hour. Refrigerate overnight.

Unmould the cheesecake by turning it upside down on a plate or board, then uprighting again.

To make the topping, put the cream in a bowl and, using an electric mixer with whisk attachment (or an electric whisk), whisk to stiff peaks. Fold in the mascarpone, icing/confectioners' sugar and vanilla extract.

Spread the topping casually over the cheesecake and top with all the berries. Dust icing/confectioners' sugar over the top before serving.

banoffee Bourbon cheesecake

This is one of those desserts that reminds me of both bananas Foster and banoffee pie. Throw in a cheesecake and you have a thoroughly fusion dessert.

400 g/14 oz. digestive biscuits/
graham crackers

75–100 g/¾–1 stick unsalted butter,
melted

800 g/1 lb. 12 oz. cream cheese

225 g/1 cup plus 1 tablespoon caster/
superfine sugar

2 eggs

50 g/½ cup plus 1 tablespoon
cornflour/cornstarch

250 ml/1 cup whipping cream

1 teaspoon vanilla extract

1 can of storebought dulce de leche
(or to make your own, see page
136)

topping

150 g/1 stick plus 1 tablespoon
unsalted butter

250 g/1 cup plus 1 tablespoon dark
brown soft sugar

200 g/1 cup caster/superfine sugar

3 bananas, cut into diagonal slices

a pinch of freshly grated nutmeg

100 ml/½ cup Bourbon

*25-cm/10-inch cake pan, greased and
baselined with parchment paper*

bamboo skewer

serves 10–12

Preheat the oven to 125°C (240°F) Gas 1.

To make the crust, crush the digestive biscuits/graham crackers until you get fine crumbs. Add the melted butter – the amount of butter you will need is variable. Test by grabbing a bit of the mixture and squeezing into your hand to make a ball, then releasing your hand. The mixture should hold its shape, but also fall apart when touched slightly. If it doesn't hold its shape, add more butter, otherwise the biscuit/cracker will dissolve into the cheesecake and you'll have no crust. If it holds its shape too well, add more biscuits/crackers to absorb the butter, otherwise your crust will be too hard.

Press the mixture into the prepared cake pan and pat down until level.

Put the cream cheese and sugar in a bowl and beat until well mixed and the sugar has dissolved.

Slowly incorporate the eggs, one at a time, beating until thoroughly combined before adding the next. Scrape the side of the bowl regularly to make sure everything is incorporated.

Sift the cornflour/cornstarch into the mixture and stir until thoroughly combined. Add the cream and vanilla extract and mix until combined. Pour the mixture into the cake pan over the crust. Add dollops of dulce de leche and swirl through the mixture a fork.

Bake in the preheated oven for 1 hour 20 minutes until the middle is slightly jiggly and the top doesn't look shiny or wet any more.

Remove from the oven and let cool in the pan for 1 hour. Refrigerate overnight.

Unmould the cheesecake by turning it upside down on a plate or board, then uprighting again.

To make the topping, put the butter and both sugars in a non-stick frying pan over medium–high heat. Cook until you get a nice, gooey caramel. Add the slices of banana and the nutmeg and cook until hot. When the mixture is bubbling, light a bamboo skewer. Immediately add the Bourbon to the bananas and light with the bamboo skewer. It should have a quick blue flame and then dissipate.

Let the topping cool before spreading over the cheesecake.

amaretto cheesecake with caramelized peaches

This is the perfect dessert to have in the evening on the tail end of summer when it starts to cool down and you want something summery but also rich enough to warm you on a breezy night. The combination of peaches and almonds is at once creamy, floral and earthy.

400 g/14 oz. amaretti biscuits/cookies

75–100 g/¾–1 stick unsalted butter, melted

800 g/1 lb. 12 oz. cream cheese

225 g/1 cup plus 1 tablespoon caster/superfine sugar

2 eggs

50 g/½ cup plus 1 tablespoon cornflour/cornstarch

250 ml/1 cup whipping cream

1 teaspoon Amaretto liqueur

topping

8 ripe peaches

85 g/⅔ stick unsalted butter

250 g/1 cup plus 1 tablespoon light brown soft sugar

50 g/3 tablespoons golden syrup

you will also need lots of ice

25-cm/10-inch cake pan, greased and baselined with parchment paper

serves 10–12

Preheat the oven to 125°C (240°F) Gas 1.

To make the crust, crush the amaretti biscuits/cookies until you get fine crumbs. Add the melted butter – the amount of butter you will need is variable. Test by grabbing a bit of the mixture and squeezing into your hand to make a ball, then releasing your hand. The mixture should hold its shape, but also fall apart when touched slightly. If it doesn't hold its shape, add more butter, otherwise the biscuit/cookie will dissolve into the cheesecake and you'll have no crust. If it holds its shape too well, add more biscuits/cookies to absorb the butter, otherwise your crust will be too hard.

Press the mixture into the prepared cake pan and pat down until level.

Put the cream cheese and sugar in a bowl and beat until well mixed and the sugar has dissolved.

Slowly incorporate the eggs, one at a time, beating until thoroughly combined before adding the next.

Sift the cornflour/cornstarch into the mixture and stir until thoroughly combined. Add the cream and Amaretto and mix until combined. Pour the mixture into the cake pan over the crust and bake in the preheated oven for 1 hour 20 minutes until the middle is slightly jiggly and the top doesn't look shiny or wet any more.

Remove from the oven and let cool in the pan for 1 hour. Refrigerate overnight.

Unmould the cheesecake by turning it upside down on a plate or board, then uprighting again.

To make the topping, fill a medium saucepan up to halfway with water and bring to a boil. Fill a bowl three quarters of the way up with cold water and ice cubes. Score a small cross on the bottom of each peach with a paring knife. Using a slotted spoon, submerge the peaches in the pan of boiling water for 15 seconds or less – until you see the skin flapping around the cross. Immediately transfer the peaches to the ice water to cool. Drain, pat dry, pull the skin off and cut into slices. Discard the stones.

Melt the butter, sugar and golden syrup in a saucepan over medium–high heat. Cook until melted, bubbling and a nice honey-brown, then add the peach slices and stir constantly – the peaches will release their juices, thinning the caramel sauce. Let cool for a few minutes, then pour gently over the cheesecake.

spiced pumpkin cheesecake

One of our beloved regulars, Felicity Spector, swears by this cheesecake. It's the quintessential autumnal dessert and has an incredible lightness despite the amount of cream cheese and cream used. I love to scatter toasted pumpkin seeds on top to add a bit of crunchiness, and if you wish to be indulgent, drizzles of caramel sauce on top will do the trick.

600 g/1 lb. 5 oz. gingernut biscuits/ cookies

75–100 g/¾–1 stick unsalted butter, melted

100 g/½ cup caster/superfine sugar

110 g/½ cup dark brown soft sugar

1½ teaspoons ground cinnamon

½ teaspoon freshly grated nutmeg

1 tablespoon ground ginger

1 teaspoon ground allspice

½ teaspoon salt

1 teaspoon vanilla extract

700 g/1 lb. 9 oz. cream cheese

3 eggs

3 tablespoons whipping cream

2 tablespoons Bourbon

425-g/15-oz. can of pumpkin purée

topping

300 ml/1⅓ cups whipping cream

60 g/⅔ cup icing/confectioners' sugar

75 g/3 oz. crystallized ginger, chopped

3 tablespoons pumpkin seeds, toasted

25-cm/10-inch cake pan, greased and baselined with parchment paper

serves 10–12

Preheat the oven to 125°C (240°F) Gas 1.

To make the crust, crush the gingernut biscuits/cookies until you get fine crumbs. Add the melted butter – the amount of butter you will need is variable. Test by grabbing a bit of the mixture and squeezing into your hand to make a ball, then releasing your hand. The mixture should hold its shape, but also fall apart when touched slightly. If it doesn't hold its shape, add more butter, otherwise the biscuit/cookie will dissolve into the cheesecake and you'll have no crust. If it holds its shape too well, add more biscuits/cookies to absorb the butter, otherwise your crust will be too hard.

Press the mixture into the prepared cake pan and pat down until level.

Put the sugar, all the spices and the vanilla extract into a large mixing bowl and stir until well combined. Add the cream cheese and beat until well mixed and the sugar has dissolved.

Slowly incorporate the eggs, one at a time, beating until thoroughly combined before adding the next. Scrape the side of the bowl regularly to make sure everything is incorporated. Stir in the whipping cream and Bourbon. Fold in the pumpkin puree until well combined.

Pour the mixture into the cake pan over the crust and bake in the preheated oven for 1 hour until the middle is slightly jiggly and the top doesn't look shiny or wet any more.

Remove from the oven and let cool in the pan for 1 hour. Refrigerate overnight.

Unmould the cheesecake by turning it upside down on a plate or board, then uprighting again.

To make the topping, put the cream and icing/confectioners' sugar in a bowl and, using an electric mixer with whisk attachment (or an electric whisk), whisk to soft peaks. Spread the topping casually over the cheesecake and top with the crystallized ginger and pumpkin seeds.

German chocolate cheesecake

Our German chocolate cake is one of our most popular flavours, but sometimes I find the dulce de leche, coconut and pecan mix pairs even better with the tanginess of cheesecake. If you can't find flaked coconut try coconut chips instead – desiccated coconut gets lost in the dulce de leche and tastes grainy. Better yet, if you can find young coconut in a specialty grocer, you can grate it and dry it in a low oven to replicate flaked.

600 g/1 lb. 5 oz. HobNobs, graham crackers or anzac biscuits

75–100 g/¾–1 stick unsalted butter, melted

800 g/1 lb. 12 oz. cream cheese

225 g/1 cup plus 1 tablespoon caster/superfine sugar

2 eggs

50 g/½ cup plus 1 tablespoon cornflour/cornstarch

250 ml/1 cup whipping cream

1 teaspoon vanilla extract

topping

Fudge Icing (see page 88)

100 g/4 oz. storebought dulce de leche (or to make your own, see method opposite – you will need a 397-g/14-oz. can of sweetened condensed milk)

5 tablespoons soft shredded coconut e.g. Baker's Angel Flake (do not replace with desiccated coconut), lightly toasted

75 g/⅔ cup pecan halves, lightly toasted and crushed

melted dark/semi-sweet chocolate, for drizzling

25-cm/10-inch cake pan, greased and baselined with parchment paper

serves 10–12

To make your own dulce de leche, put the can of condensed milk in a large saucepan and cover with water. Bring to a boil and let simmer over low heat for 4 hours, continually adding hot water as needed so that the can is always covered with water. (You can do multiple cans simultaneously, and unopened cans can be stored in a cupboard for up to 3 months.) Let the can cool, then open up. You should have a dark caramelized milk. (Store any opened dulce de leche in an airtight container in fridge for up to 2 months.)

Preheat the oven to 125°C (240°F) Gas 1.

To make the crust, crush the biscuits/cookies until you get fine crumbs. Add the melted butter – the amount of butter you will need is variable. Test by grabbing a bit of the mixture and squeezing into your hand to make a ball, then releasing your hand. The mixture should hold its shape, but also fall apart when touched slightly. If it doesn't hold its shape, add more butter otherwise the biscuit/cracker will dissolve into the cheesecake and you'll have no crust. If it holds its shape too well, add more biscuits/crackers to absorb the butter, otherwise your crust will be too hard.

Press the mixture into the prepared cake pan and pat down until level.

Put the cream cheese and sugar in a bowl and beat until well mixed and the sugar has dissolved.

Slowly incorporate the eggs, one at a time, beating until thoroughly combined before adding the next. Scrape the side of the bowl regularly to make sure everything is incorporated. Sift the cornflour/cornstarch into the mixture and stir until thoroughly combined.

Add the cream and vanilla extract and mix until combined. Pour the mixture into the cake pan over the crust and bake in the preheated oven for 1 hour until the middle is slightly jiggly and the top doesn't look shiny or wet any more.

Remove from the oven and let cool in the pan for 1 hour. Refrigerate overnight.

Unmould the cheesecake by turning it upside down on a plate or board, then uprighting again.

Spread a layer of Fudge Icing over the cheesecake. Warm the dulce de leche slightly in a microwave for 20 seconds, and drizzle over the fudge icing in nice big dollops. Sprinkle the coconut, pecans and some melted chocolate all over.

chocolate peanut butter swirl cheesecake

A quick web search for a Chocolate Peanut Butter Cheesecake will result in thousands of recipes. I hope this one comes near the top of the heap, as we tempered the sweetness a bit to allow the chocolate and peanut butter to really shine through. I've recommended honey-roasted peanuts for the top but if you want to be adventurous, salty, spiced peanuts would add an interesting counterpoint, and is a very Michelin-star thing to do.

crust

400 g/14 oz. finely crushed Chocolate Peanut Butter Biscotti (see page 27)

75–100 g/¾–1 stick unsalted butter, melted

800 g/1 lb. 12 oz. cream cheese

225 g/1 cup plus 1 tablespoon caster/superfine sugar

2 eggs

50 g/½ cup plus 1 tablespoon cornflour/cornstarch

250 ml/1 cup whipping cream

1 teaspoon vanilla extract

200 g/7 oz. dark/semi-sweet chocolate, melted

topping

Fudge Icing (see page 88)

as much peanut butter as you like (chunky or smooth)

chocolate curls, to decorate

honey-roasted peanuts, to decorate

25-cm/10-inch cake pan, greased and baselined with parchment paper

serves 10–12

Preheat the oven to 125°C (240°F) Gas 1.

To make the crust, crush the Chocolate Peanut Butter Biscotti until you get fine crumbs. Add the melted butter – the amount of butter you will need is variable. Test by grabbing a bit of the mixture and squeezing into your hand to make a ball, then releasing your hand. The mixture should hold its shape, but also fall apart when touched slightly. If it doesn't hold its shape, add more butter, otherwise the biscotti will dissolve into the cheesecake and you'll have no crust. If it holds its shape too well, add more biscotti to absorb the butter, otherwise your crust will be too hard.

Press the mixture into the prepared cake pan and pat down until level.

Put the cream cheese and sugar in a bowl and beat until well mixed and the sugar has dissolved.

Slowly incorporate the eggs, one at a time, beating until thoroughly combined before adding the next.

Sift the cornflour/cornstarch into the mixture and stir until thoroughly combined. Add the cream and vanilla extract and mix until combined. Transfer half the mixture to a separate bowl and fold in the melted chocolate.

Pour both mixtures into the cake pan over the crust and swirl with fork to create a marbled effect. Bake in the preheated oven for 1 hour until the middle is slightly jiggly and the top doesn't look shiny or wet any more.

Remove from the oven and let cool in the pan for 1 hour. Refrigerate overnight.

Unmould the cheesecake by turning it upside down on a plate or board, then uprighting again.

Spread a layer of Fudge Icing over the cheesecake. Warm the peanut butter slightly and spoon over the fudge icing in nice big dollops. Swirl with fork to create a marbled effect. Decorate with chocolate curls and honey-roasted peanuts.

ideas for tea parties

Breakfast

Assam breakfast tea

Earl Grey tea

Granola Bars (page 32)

Almond Cherry Muffins (page 48)

Blueberry Streusel Muffins (page 47)

Doughnut Muffins (page 51)

Orange Cranberry Scones (page 43)

Apple Bourbon Pecan Cake (page 104)

Lavender Shortbread (page 23)

Father's day

Ultimate Chocolate Chip Cookies (page 16)

Golden Bourbon Pecan Custard Pie (page 71)

Apple Bourbon Pecan Cake (page 104)

Doughnut Muffins (page 51)

Sea Salt Caramels (page 60)

Baileys Marshmallows (page 59)

Killer Valrhona Brownies (page 35)

Mother's day

The Ultimate Coconut Cream Pie (page 68)

The Renee (page 110)

The Ultimate Afternoon Tea Scone (page 40)

Vanilla Cheesecake with Berries (page 128)

Foolproof Vanilla Macarons (page 56)

Sea Salt Caramels (page 60)

Mocha Financiers (page 52)

Nutty Lemon Biscotti (page 28)

Valentine's day

Raspberry Meringues (page 55)

Raspberry Marshmallows (page 59)

Red Velvet Cake (page 97)

The Ultimate Afternoon Tea Scone (page 40)

Milk Chocolate Sesame Cream Tart
with Glazed Cherries (page 75)

Killer Valrhona Brownies (page 35)

Christmas

Baileys Marshmallows (page 59)

Gingerbread Guinness Cake with Poached Pears
& Cream Cheese Icing (page 121)

Banoffee Bourbon Cheesecake (page 131)

Leftovers Trifle (page 106)

Poached pear & Frangipane Tart (page 72)

Golden Bourbon Pecan Custard Pie (page 71)

Almond Financiers (page 52)

Lemon Verbena Semolina Cookies (page 20)

Baby shower

Vanilla Coconut Cake with Lemon Curd &
Cheesecake Filling (page 113)

Foolproof Vanilla and Raspberry Macarons (page 56)

The Ultimate Afternoon Tea Scone (page 40)

Red Velvet Cake (page 97)

Nutty Lemon Biscotti (page 28)

Belgian Blondies (page 36)

Triple Chocolate Cake (page 114)

Mocha Financiers (page 52)

index

credits & acknowledgments

This book would not have come to fruition without the dedicated work of Céline Hughes, Alison Starling, Steve Painter, and the team at Ryland Peters & Small. Special thanks go to my dad Lee Stone, my sister Von Kay, and my brother-in-law Paul Kay who raised me. Bea's of Bloomsbury would not have existed without the encouragement and support of Omar Khan; to Colleen Jolly who designed the logo, and Ting Ting Zhang and William Tan for christening the name Bea's of Bloomsbury; to Kulan Mills who is like an uncle to BOB; to Kristina Johansson who was there from when BOB was just an idea; to Lucy Henry for helping shape BOB in the beginning; to Beth Davies who continues to redefine BOB year after year; to the pastry team at BOB who took care of the roost while I was busy writing; to the front of house staff at BOB who've always managed to add great personality to the place even if they won't let me have coffee!; to Renee Senne who gave me my first break and taught me almost everything I know; to Regis Cursan who taught me everything else; to Shuna Lydon whose generosity of spirit revives a love of pastry in times high and low; to Go Sugimoto whose art and design have influenced BOB time and time again; to Anette Moldvaer and James Hoffmann who have been so supportive; to all of the regulars at BOB who have supported us and helped us to make BOB better for them; to James Shirley, who's been an invaluable supporter; to Shafeena for her everlasting support; to Andre Dang for his support of the book; to my friends Sarah, Lisa, Terron and Mike who manage to make it there when I need them the most; and finally to my husband Franz Schinagl who has put up with everything and more and I love him for it.

The publisher would like to thank the following people for the kind loan of props used in the book:

For tiles:
R.I.M tile & mosaic boutique
Tel: +44(0)20 7376 5820
www.rimdesign.co.uk

For plain metallic wallpapers:
Altfield
Tel: +44(0)20 7351 5893
www.altfield.com

For Florence Broadhurst design wallpapers and fabrics:
Borderline Fabrics
Tel: +44(0)20 7823 3567;
www.borderlinefabrics.com

For damask fabrics:
Lelièvre
Tel: +44(0)20 7352 4798;
www.lelievre.eu

For Tina Tsang cake stands and tea set on page 41, 87, 90, 144:
Undergrowth Design
www.undergrowthdesign.com

For small tile on page 61:
Peter Ibruegger
peteribruegger.com